The Seven Human Needs

*A Practical Guide to Finding Harmony
and Balance in Everyday Life*

By Gudjon Bergmann

The Seven Human Needs:
A Practical Guide to Finding Harmony and Balance in Every Day Life
by Gudjon Bergmann

Published by Hanuman
Hafnafjordur, Iceland
gudjon@gbergmann.is
Tel: +354-690-1818
www.sevenhumanneeds.com

LCCN (Library of Congress Catalog Number) - 2006-903988
ISBN: 1-4196-3666-9

For additional copies visit: www.sevenhumanneeds.com, www.booksurge.com or www.amazon.com.

POD / Booksurge LLC – Printed in the USA

Table of contents

Gratitude

This book is dedicated to the memory of my father, Gudlaugur Bergmann, who was born on October 20, 1938 and died on December 27, 2004. He lived his life to the fullest, with energy and passion, contemplated the divine and worked enthusiastically to secure sustainable development. May the memory of his life be an inspiration to all those who knew him. May his soul live eternally.

Affectionate gratitude goes to my wife, Johanna, for her loving support and encouragement in my endeavors, and to my son Daniel and stepdaughter Bara, for always being there for me.

To my family, my mother Gudrun, my brothers, grandmother and other relatives, I want to extend gratitude from the level of my soul. My family has nurtured me and stood by me all my life and supported the choices I have made.

My deepest appreciation and admiration goes to my teachers, Yogi Shanti Desai and Shri Yogi Hari, who have given me profound insights into the spiritual dimensions of life. They serve as divine inspiration to all those who come into contact with them.

I would like to thank Stephen Pierce and his staff at the seminar *Publishing for Profits*, for their role in this publication and Amazon/Booksurge LLC for rendering a valuable service to self-published authors like myself.

I would also like to extend a special thank-you to the authors I recommend in the resource section of this book. Their books, audio programs, seminars and teachings have enriched my life in many ways.

I would also like to thank all my students through the years. They have given me inspiration through their enthusiasm, and the financial means to keep on teaching and writing.

Last but not least I would like to show appreciation to the deepest part of my soul. My ego has tried to get out of the way and let the divine spark shine through while writing this book and I apologize for any contamination on my part.

Introduction

"To be prepared is half the victory."
- Miguel De Cervantes

The Balancing Act Called LIFE

"There is only one corner of the universe you can be certain
of improving, and that's your own self."
- Aldous Huxley

You have within you all the elements of security, excitement, creativity, individual strength, love, expression, contribution, wisdom, growth and spirituality. These elements are meant to be extracted, balanced and utilized for a harmonious and happy life. The philosophy of the seven human needs is designed to bring an awareness to a timeless truth; that there are seven very different and yet interdependent *needs* that every human being must fulfill and balance. These are not mere wants, longings or preferences, but undeniable needs, and everyone must find a way to balance the seven, if they want to develop health, happiness and peace of mind. The model is really not my invention, but rather it is the culmination of experience, research and integration between different disciplines and modes of inquiry. It's a practical philosophy that anyone can apply.

I started looking for answers because I noticed that people in general could be doing well in one area of their life, but be totally out of balance in other areas. In my teens I was catapulted to the forefront of the New Age revolution in Iceland, where my parents were in the lead, and from that experience I learned very much about human behavior. One thing I realized was that many people in the New Age movement (including myself) were full to the brim with mystical knowledge and spiritual awareness, but some could not sustain themselves financially, many didn't take very good care of their health and a still larger number failed in their relationships.

My search for an answer to this human dilemma of imbalance has lasted for over fifteen years; it has taken much effort and is still going strong. In my research I have read hundreds of personal development books, I have studied spirituality, psychology, philosophy, goal setting, health, money and personal development. Each book I have read has contributed a piece to the puzzle. I have listened to audio programs, gone to seminars; I have studied and practiced yoga for over ten years, meditated, interviewed psychics, psychiatrists, psychologists and read about astrology. I have also gained incredible insight into the workings of the human mind through my smoking cessation seminars, where for the last nine years I have taught hundreds of people to use their minds to free themselves from nicotine addiction. All this information, and more, has been integrated into my work to some degree.

The trouble I see with much of the circulating self-development material is that it tends to emphasize one need at the cost of another. Body builders emphasize health, psychologists emphasize emotions, entrepreneurs emphasize money and spiritual masters emphasize meditation, to name a few. When people find their strength in life they tend to focus all their energy in that one direction. This is natural. That kind of determined focus is surely the reason for many great successes in life, but one area should not be pursued at the expense of another in such a way that an otherwise whole person feels fragmented. I have tried the fragmented approach and it does not work.

Many authors of the above mentioned self-development material have gotten themselves into a dilemma because they promise happiness as a result of their approach. Get rich quick and be happy, build your body for life and be happy, find love in a relationship and be happy. But this is only partly true; life is not just meditation, just money, just health, just emotional relationships, just learning etc. Life is a healthy balance of all these needs and more.

The principals in this book are based on: the *chakra* system (see epilogue), the idea of harmony found in the texts of Plato and Aristotle, the hierarchy of needs by Abraham Maslow, the six human emotional needs taught by Anthony Robbins and the integral model written about by Ken Wilber. The philosophy of the seven human needs draws inspiration from many other sources and yet it remains simple and practical in its application.

It's a Circus Act

"Everyone thinks of changing the world,
but no one thinks of changing himself."
- Tolstoy

Before we delve deeper into each of the seven human needs I would like you to entertain a metaphor in your mind by visioning a popular circus act. The aim of the performer is to balance plates on top of long sticks. He starts by spinning one plate on top of a single stick. When the first plate has been balanced he moves on to the next and so on. His aim is to keep the plates balanced and spinning and to balance as many plates as possible without any of the previous plates falling down and breaking. This is a continual process, changing between focus and overview. The performer steps in towards the stick in order to balance each plate with his total concentration, and then steps out to get an overview of his progress. If he finds that any of the plates need his attention he moves in and gives that one plate his total focus until it is balanced again. He then steps out to get an overview once more. If none of the plates need his attention he can start spinning a new plate on a new stick. It's a continual process. It is very important to note that the performer cannot focus on the overview and focus on a single stick at the same time. Instead he switches his attention back and forth.

After getting to know the seven human needs, a similar balancing act can become a central part of your life. While working to find balance and harmony you must continually switch between focused attention on one area and an overview. Just like the circus performer you need to get an overview to see where things are out of balance. Once you see clearly where the imbalance is located, you can step in and focus all your attention on balancing that part of your life. Then you step out, get an overview again, find another part of life that is out of balance, step in and correct that, and on it goes. It's a *continual process*, because things never seem to stay balanced on their own for very long. If at any point you get sidetracked in your concentration (focus on one area for too long without regard for the other areas) or overview (watch the imbalance without taking the necessary steps to correct it) one or more areas of you life will suffer the consequences. This is called continual self-awareness or continuous self-study. The difference between you and the circus performer is that you only have to focus on seven important areas – the performer is paid to always aim for more.

By reading and applying the material in this book, the idea of this balancing act will become clearer.

The middle path of balance and harmony

"Happiness is when what you think, what you say, and what you do are in harmony."
- Gandhi

The principals of balance and harmony have been with human kind for thousands of years. The master philosopher Aristotle is one of many who have recommended the middle path in life. Here is an excerpt from Will Durant's book *The Story of Philosophy*:

> *"Aristotle said that the qualities of character can be arranged in triads, in each of which the first and last qualities will be extremes and vices, and the middle quality a virtue of excellence. So between cowardice and rashness is courage; between stinginess and extravagance is liberality; between sloth and greed is ambition; between humility and pride is modesty; between secrecy and loquacity, honesty; between moroseness and buffoonery, good humor; between quarrelsomeness and flattery, friendship; between Hamlet's indecisiveness and Quixote's impulsiveness is self-control."*

It is very important to note that each successive need includes the previous need. This means that within the need for excitement there is an embedded need for security. For most human beings security comes first, so any attempts at finding excitement will have to be secure, but in an exciting way. For example going to the movies; it's a safe practice that can also be exciting, but you will furthermore learn that even though the needs are interdependent, they are also independent of each other in many ways, and people can repress or disregard one or more of the needs, while in an excessive pursuit of another. The balancing act between security and excitement is indeed hard to master. So is the balancing of individual strength and the need for love and relationships. Our creator seems to have had a real sense of humor when he/she/it embedded these seemingly conflicting and yet interdependent needs within each and every one of us.

Having emphasized the balancing act I want to note that it's alright to specialize. Each of us has different strengths and weaknesses. You can be an expert on money, emotions, science or meditation. Be sure to pursue your desired path with most of your energy. But don't forget to pay some attention to the other needs. Make sure you find balance. I will discuss this in greater detail later on in the book.

We are all looking for balance from the time we learn to walk, until we are given more responsibility or heavier burdens, and then we must find balance again. It's a continual process as I have already mentioned. I was reminded of this while watching my three year old son Daniel carrying a backpack down the stairs in our apartment. Although he is stable when he walks down the stairs without a backpack, he had trouble with balancing in almost every step when he decided to carry a relatively heavy backpack and I had to assist him so he wouldn't fall. With time and practice he will not need my help while walking down the stairs with that particular backpack, but by then he'll probably want to carry something heavier. It's the same with all of us. Everything is hard before it becomes easy - we all want to grow - and practice makes perfect. Keep that in mind while you're reading and applying the information contained in this book.

How to Use This Book

"If you know that you don't know, that is a great beginning.
Then it is possible for you to know."
- Socrates

When I started to lay out the framework for the seven human needs, I was looking for a balance between health, happiness and peace of mind (which incidentally was also the title of a book I wrote and published in Iceland in 2004). The search for that foundation in life is a powerful driving force and motivator, and I am not easily deferred even though I have not achieved everything I set out to do yet. In reality I don't see myself becoming a fully whole (or holy) human being in this lifetime. I am pressing for progress, not perfection. Setting my sights on the moon means I'll never end up with a handful of dust. My goal is to be practical and teach in a manner that most everyone can relate to. Therefore my emphasis while writing this manual is to be pragmatic.

If you are to know anything about the workings of the human mind it should be this: *you become what you think about most of the time.* What you focus on expands in your life! There are so many things going on in your surroundings that you can only notice those things that you find either repulsive/depressive or interesting/appealing/exciting. Both get equal attention. This principal can be found within most spiritual and philosophical traditions. Based on this information my book is set up in an easy to read and easy to follow manner. It is designed to activate your awareness and your subconscious mind through repetition.

The Challenge

"Repetition is the mother of skill."
- Anthony Robbins

Here is the challenge: *read about one need every day (seven needs – seven days a week), especially the practical advice, questions and affirmations, for the next few weeks or months and see what happens.* Cultivate awareness and notice both the visible and subtle changes that take place within you and your environment. In this lifetime you can only strive to control three things, what you think, what you say and what you do. So, decide to take control of you own life and see where it leads you. Embrace this challenge and get to know yourself and your needs in a more complete way. This book is not meant to change everything in your life all at once, but if you follow the instructions by reading about one need every day for the next few weeks or even months, use the affirmations and answer the questions at the end of each chapter – I promise – you *will* see positive changes happen in your life.

Having someone to share this experience with can make it even more meaningful and may help you to create more of a lasting change. You can share it with a spouse, a friend or a relative, for example. You can read about the needs together, talk about the things in your life that correspond with the needs, answer the questions in the back of each chapter together and discuss the answers.

Stages of learning

"Just as iron rusts from disuse,
even so does inaction spoil the intellect."
- Leonardo Da Vinci

To help you orient yourself in this process let me remind you of the four stages of learning. The first stage of learning has been called unconscious incompetent (you don't know that you don't know). Many people are situated at this first stage in numerous areas of their life. It has also been called the bliss of ignorance, but it's not bliss, it's just ignorance. The second stage is called conscious incompetent (you know that you don't know). It's probably the hardest part of the process but also the most rewarding. When people find out that they don't know something, they have two options, try to forget about it or do something to change the situation. If a person decides to change it can lead to the third stage which has been called conscious competent (you know that you know – you are very aware of everything that you have just learned or changed and must focus intently on it so you don't forget). The third level is the level of intentional and continuous practice and focus. The fourth stage is called unconscious competent (you know it so well that you don't even have to think about it – it has become part of who you are). This has also been called the bliss of knowledge and rightly so.

It's like learning to ride a bicycle. At first you don't know that there is such a thing as a bicycle (stage one). Then when you get old enough to recognize bicycles you realize that you don't know how to ride one (stage two). Then you practice and practice. You're not very good to begin with and have to focus intently on mastering the bicycle (stage three). But, when you know how to ride a bike, you never forget. It becomes a part of who you are (stage four).

Recognize where you are located within these four stages while you read about the needs. Knowing where you are gives you a better chance to move forward and make the changes necessary.

The design of each chapter

"The life which is unexamined is not worth living."
- ***Plato***

Each chapter is specifically designed to have the maximum positive effect on you and your life. The chapters are long enough to be of use, but short enough so that you can find time to read about one need a day (and maybe read something else as well).

In the beginning of each chapter you will find an overview about a particular need. Next you will find general information about what the need may look like when it is out of balance. I have probably not included everything that can go wrong, but just enough information so that you will get the big picture. Balancing the human needs will mean first finding what is *out of balance,* then finding balance within *each need* and then achieving *harmony between all the needs.*

Close to the end of each chapter you will find practical advice. I want you to realize that the advice given in this book comes as a result of many centuries worth of accumulated human knowledge and experience I have *gathered* from books, audio programs, seminars and real life situations. Even so, I will encourage you to continue and read more, listen to audio programs and go to seminars. If you like the advice, take it. If not, find better ways by tapping into your own creativity.

Now even though it may seem tempting, *don't try to change everything at once.* First comes awareness – then comes change. Take baby steps - decide to do something small but consistent to advance *every day* and tackle one area at a time. The law of incremental improvement, by speaker and author Brian Tracy, will work in your favor. He says that if you become 0.1 % better at something every day, and only work at it five days a week, that will translate into 2 % improvement each month, and that in turn will translate into 24% improvement in a year, just by doing something small but consistent every day to get better and better.

Asking better questions will lead to getting better answers, in most cases, so close to the end of each chapter you will find questions that can help you grow, that is to say, if you answer them honestly. If you read about one need each day (recommended), you can answer the questions mentally, but be sure to stop every now and then and *write your answers down* on a piece of paper. If you are only going to read the book once, be sure to do this the first time around – because, like teacher and lecturer Glenn Dietzel puts it, writing is the doing part of thinking. Let me repeat that, *writing is the doing part of thinking.* Once you write it down, it will become more real to you.

At the very end of every chapter about a particular need you will find affirmations related to that need. These are statements in the first person singular (a formula closely related to declarations and incantations) designed to have the maximum effect on your subconscious mind so that you can integrate the material faster. Repeat the affirmations to yourself on a regular basis, either aloud or mentally, or meditate on their meaning.

But remember that only action leads to change, so every day you should make an effort to put the affirmations into action.

In the back of the book you will also find further resources - books, seminars, programs etc. Many of the books and audio programs recommended touch on various subjects within the seven human needs and so you may find the same books or audio programs being recommended in more than area because of the scope of their material.

Prioritize your resources

"Tomorrow I plan to work, work, from early until late.
In fact I have so much to do that I shall spend
the first three hours in prayer."
- Martin Luther

Time is the only resource you cannot save. You can't tuck it away under your pillow and store it for a rainy day. Time can only be spent or invested. Now, even though it cannot be saved, time is the main resource you use to divide your attention between the seven human needs in order to find balance. Everyone gets the same 24 hours a day. Everyone spends or invests these hours in a fashion they see fit. People only invest time in projects they think are *important*. As you read and realize how important these human needs are you can start utilizing the limited resources of time, money and energy to find balance and harmony within life.

Many of the concepts in this book may seem pretty basic and you might find your self uttering phrases under your breath like: "I know this." If that happens, why don't you stop for a moment and think: "Do I really know?" "Am I living the idea?" "Am I using it?" "Is it already a part of my life?" If you

answer that it isn't a part of your life and you're not a living example of its potency, it probably wouldn't hurt you to read the idea again ... and maybe again, until it becomes your second nature.

The First Wave of Needs

*"He who conquers others is strong:
he who conquers himself is mighty."*
- Lao-tzu

The 1st Need

The Need for Security

"The richest person is the one
who is contented with what he has."
- Robert C. Savage

To understand the need for security, it is necessary to split it into two distinctive parts. One is our need for physical survival (health, food and shelter) and the other is a need for security through other needs (secure social status, relationships, self-security and so on). Since the need for security is the primal foundation in all human behavior, it is the need that invariably gets the most attention in life. To start the evaluation process, let's take a short look at what some of these security factors are and how they affect your daily life. Remember that the aim here is to find balance.

Survival – Everyone needs food and a roof over their head. In western society money has become synonymous with security. We work for money to pay for food, housing and clothing, but we also do it to secure our social status and buy things we really don't need. According to ancient philosophy there are three kinds of suffering, each with real and illusory aspects and they are all connected to the need for survival, but their illusory aspects go beyond mere survival. The real aspect of the first is not having the basic necessities of life; the illusory aspect is not having the things that others have. The real aspect of the second source of suffering is physical diseases and pain; the illusory aspect is minor physical complaints which are magnified by imagination or fear. The third source is having an abundance of everything but worrying about sustaining it. Like the quote in the beginning of this chapter implies *(the richest person is the one who is contented with what he has)*, the state of mind you are in is very important.

If they really wanted to, most people could probably accumulate a desired amount of wealth through saving and investing, and spend more time pursuing the other needs. That would result in a more balanced and fulfilled life. But, in reality this is not the case. Most people struggle with money, and unfortunately many have made negative mental associations when it comes to the subject of money. Events in their childhood may have left financial scars on their minds that are slow to heal. The ancient truth that says *you become what you think about most of the time* has equal effects in the area of finances as in other areas. Thought patterns govern your relationship with money. If you don't take time to master your finances you will invariably tend to be negative when you think about money. And since much of your life revolves around security and much of security is related to money, you really don't want to be negative about the concept of money; unless you want to be negative and fearful for the rest of your life.

There are many ways to become financially independent. If you create many useless, unreal and artificial needs to fulfill in life, then you need a large income or acquire a large net worth. But if you simplify life, you will only need a small income or net worth to be fulfilled. Both work equally well. However, you cannot give what you don't have. Another reason to become wealthy is to contribute to others. Think about the motives behind your accumulation of money and stay detached. Don't let your money own you, *own your* money instead. Try comparing the steady paycheck with your earning ability and see which one gives you more security in the long run. Ask and answer this question: How much is enough?

Everyone knows that money is far from being the most important thing in life. Money will not make you happy, it can't buy you love and it will not give you peace of mind. But money is very important where it counts. Just be sure that you have enough, so that you do have time to pursue the other six needs. Money is a means to an end, not an end in itself. According to ancient philosophy it is the duty of a householder to be prosperous so that he does not become a burden on society.

But, even if you do everything you can to acquire financial independence, you cannot control the environment, so it is also wise to try and develop a trusting mindset when it comes to money. I love this story which is attributed to the TM founder (Transcendental Meditation) Maharishi Mahesh. He was preparing a peace ceremony for a large crowd with his disciples. When the planning was done someone asked: "But Maharishi, where is the money coming from?" He answered: "From wherever it is at the moment."

Health - According to yoga master Swami Sivananda *health is the greatest wealth*. Your body is your greatest property. Once you start to loose your health, all other wealth becomes secondary. If you won a million dollars (or your currency) in the lottery and then shortly after you lost your eyesight and the doctors told you that you could get it back in a surgery that would cost a million dollars, would you hesitate to make the trade? Of course you wouldn't.

Our need for security demands that we find health and harmony. Health is your source of energy; if you have energy you can pursue all the other needs with much more enthusiasm. Swami Vishnu-Devananda (Sivanandas disciple) recommends five pillars that one should balance to find and maintain optimum health.

1. *Proper exercise (balance between strength, stamina and flexibility).*
2. *Proper diet (simple and clean – something you can digest, assimilate and excrete easily).*
3. *Proper breathing (deep diaphragmic breathing).*
4. *Proper rest and relaxation.*
5. *Meditation and positive thinking.*

As you can see, it would be wise to follow all of these recommendations if one wishes to maintain a state of health and harmony for any extended period of time. But in order to steer clear of the narcissistic tendencies often connected with body building and fitness enthusiasts, it is good to keep in mind that eventually the body will whither away and die. In a prelude to the *Bhagavad-Gita*, it is said that the greatest mystery of life is that *no man believes he will die* even if he sees others dying all around him. You can stay healthy by following the five principles outlined here, but don't obsess over your health. A moderate amount of vanity and self-respect will serve you, but steer clear of narcissism, for that rarely leads to balance.

Social security – One of the biggest reasons for the formation of families, tribes, cities and countries is our need for security. In every society the need for security is still the biggest reason for cohesion. In the years to come, more people will hopefully see that the world could be a better place if social cohesion were to become a world wide phenomenon. The truth is simple: *We all need each other in the global village.* That kind of realization could actually bring on world peace but it's not likely to happen while we have poverty, hunger and illiteracy in the world, for under those circumstances social and personal security is severely undermined.

The purpose of this book is personal growth and transformation – which eventually may lead to global transformation. Start with yourself and continue from there. Take a look at your own social foundations. What is your relationship like with your family, friends, society, spouse and children like? A broken link within relations to your family or friends could for example create a subconscious sense of insecurity without your direct awareness. Such insecurity could subtly damage your need for loving emotions and relationships (something we will focus on in more detail later).

Religion for many people is a source of security and meaning in this life (and the next). In fact you might find that the need for security can be the most important driving force behind many of the so-called organized religions. Look at the fundamentalist religions in war-torn areas, poor countries and poor neighborhoods. People are drawn to the religious zealots because they are looking for security, a way out of the chaos. The need for security may be the driving force behind more behaviors in our lives than we would like to admit.

Science – The structure of our society and the foundation of our work in the world today is primarily based on modern scientific knowledge and achievement. We have cars, computers, the internet, mobile phones, kitchen appliances, televisions, machinery for food production and the list goes on. It would seem like a good idea to have some basic knowledge of how science works so that we can function better in the world.

The worldview of science may be limited to the sphere of the material world, but since most of us live in that world most of the time, it would be foolish to dismiss the great progress of science in all human arenas. The scientific discoveries of our time have created more security for more people than at any other time in human history. In the hands of morally integral, compassionate and caring people, science is a blessing and gives us a firm foundation of security and trust.

Nature – Securing the protection of our environment has little or nothing to do with environmental protection as I see it. In reality the so called environmental protection should be called *human* protection. The Earth will survive even if we keep polluting, but our children will suffer and their children may not live at all if we don't start doing our part to protect ourselves by conserving and protecting the environment. Working to find harmony and balance between man and nature is one of the most important and pressing tasks facing humanity today, first and foremost to secure the survival of our species. Many people feel that their security is threatened by excessive polluting and react accordingly with anger and outrage, but working for harmonious and balanced relations between humans first, and then with nature, is the only way to secure the environment in the long term, and in turn, the future of man kind.

Out of Balance

Imbalances are clearly visible when it comes to this need. Being caught in the rat race, spending all your time pursuing material wealth or success, focusing only on making a living without regard to any other need is one form of imbalance. There are also the extreme polarities of excess and deficiency; excessive greed versus poverty; narcissistic and excessive health endeavors versus obesity or anorexia; scientific phobia versus complete faith in science to the exclusion of everything else; condoning external pollution versus reverting to ancient tribal consciousness. Remember the example Aristotle gave. Your faults may actually be your greatest strengths, either in excess or deficiency. These are just a few examples of the imbalances that can be connected to this need. Just remember to watch out for those excessive and deficient pursuits. Both can be equally damaging.

Practical advice

1. Build and maintain the five pillars of health:

    a) Exercise at least three to four times a week. Do something you love to do - or learn to love it. Make it a habit and make that habit your master. Your body was made to move.

    b) Learn to breathe deeply. You can do it through yoga, acting, singing or any other way you choose. Use the energy created through deep breathing for greater endurance in life.

    c) Balance your diet. Answer the following questions (really think about this):

- Why do I eat?
- Is it for optimum nutrition or other reasons?
- When do I eat?

· Do I eat most of the food I consume in the beginning of the day or in the evening?

· How much energy do I need just before I go to sleep?

· What will my quality of sleep be like if my digestive system is working hard?

· How do I eat?

· Do I sit down and chew my food or do I always eat on the run?

· Am I distracted or concentrated?

· Do I stop eating when I am full or do I continue?

· What do I eat?

· Do I really know what is good for me?

· Can I tell which foods are unhealthy and bad for me?

· How can I balance my diet and have fun doing it?

I could go on an on. Continue, ask and answer more questions in this area. *Really think!* You know all the answers if you think about it.

d) Relax. Take a course and learn a relaxation technique, buy a relaxation CD or find constructive ways to unwind (as opposed to common ways of "relaxing" that have negative side effects, i.e. smoking, drinking alcohol, watching TV, etc.) There is a great difference between being lazy and being relaxed. You have drained your energy after a lazy spell; while relaxation gives you lots of energy. Shri Chinmoy says: "Relaxation is a change of activity." Contemplate that. Relaxation is the cooling system for your body/mind. Use it every day. Get a good night's sleep. A well respected psychiatrist in Iceland claims that many of the drugs people take, such as painkillers and mood altering substances, are due to a restless sleep or lack of sleep. Deep dreamless sleep is crucial. Reduce the intake of exciting mental images and ideas (i.e. don't watch too much

T.V.) and use relaxation techniques before you go to bed if you have trouble sleeping.

e) **Cultivate positive thinking.** Look for solutions, not problems. Find ways to look on the bright side of life (listen to the Monty Python song *Always Look on the Bright Side of Life* if you can't find any other means... it's certain to bring a smile to your face).

2. Use several ways to measure your health

Measure your weight, strength, endurance, blood pressure, flexibility, dental situation and digestion, to name a few. The best way to stay healthy is to balance all of these and more.

a) **Weight.** Maintaining a balanced weight is probably one of the most beneficial ways to stay healthy. But it is not the only measure of health. Thin people can be as unhealthy as fat people. Just be sure not to obsess to the point of losing your peace of mind over your physical appearance so long as you are healthy.

b) **Healthy muscles.** Strength and flexibility are two sides of the same coin. Healthy muscles are strong and relaxed. Unhealthy muscles are often hard and sensitive. Find a balance between strength and flexibility. If you are able to sit still with a straight back for an extended period of time (during meditation for example) and yet able to use your strength for daily activities, it means that your muscles are likely to be fairly healthy.

c) **Physical stamina and endurance.** You can take all kinds of tests to find out the level of your stamina. Talk to a doctor or go to a local health club to get your stamina measured.

d) **Check you blood pressure regularly.** Maintaining a healthy weight, strong and flexible muscles and physical stamina does not ensure that your blood pressure is optimal.

e) **Take care of your teeth.** Yes, studies show that there is a direct relation between dental care and longevity.

f) Digestion. You are not only what you eat. You are what you *digest* and *assimilate*. Take care of your digestive system and it will take care of you. Eat a high fiber diet, don't overeat and exercise regularly. Regular excretion, fasting and cleansing are also beneficial.

3. Drive safely.

Why is this recommendation here? Because so many lives are cut short due to unsafe driving. You can't control other people in traffic but you can do your best to avoid accidents by driving safely.

4. Go for regular medical checkups!

Use the medical and scientific knowledge that has been acquired by mankind through the ages. Even if you are more inclined to use natural remedies, modern medical technology is amazing and can help you prevent illness as well as diagnose an illness at its early stages.

5. Plan your finances

Learn to earn, save and invest money. There are many ways to do this. Read some of the books on finances recommended in the resource section at the end of this book. Find a financial advisor or take a workshop on how to manage your finances. If you don't learn to manage your money, your money will manage you. Managing and planning your finances can help you reach a level of security that gives you a strong foundation for pursuing the other needs mentioned in this book.

6. Work to stabilize and secure your society

There are many ways to get involved. Politics is the most obvious way, but that's not for everyone. Think of the ways in which you could contribute to your family and society to further secure and stabilize your surroundings. While contemplating what you can do, you might discover that the best place to start is within yourself. Try to find peace and security within and work from there.

7. Build and preserve your social support group
Your social support group can consist of friends, family, your spouse, your co-workers or any organizations you belong to. The need for security is so great that everyone must have a backup, a person or persons they can turn to in an hour of need, someone they can trust. The best way to earn trust is to give it. Look out for others and help those in need. This will ensure that you have backup when you need it. As a bonus, this approach to life can bring you joy and happiness. People who isolate themselves from family, friends and society can feel an immense lack of security and not know where it stems from. Having money and material luxury will not compensate for the lack of a social support group.

8. Help to protect the environment
Working for environmental protection is really an acronym for working for the continued survival of the human species, for the survival of your children and their children. Speaking in Biblical terms we cannot let our children suffer "the sins of the fathers." The threat is very real and imminent. Read more about it and adopt a new state of mind. The most catastrophic notion that people have, is that what *they do* doesn't make a difference. Turn that belief around and start doing something, anything you can do to make a difference. Live with awareness, spread that awareness and you will find that slowly but surely a person

who starts making changes at home can make a real difference in the world.

9. Count your blessings

This is an age-old advice and has become a cliché of sorts. But why do phrases become clichés? Because in most cases there is some truth to them; and they have been used over and over again to explain that truth. Counting your blessings is a practice that can greatly enhance your feeling of security. Everyone who is alive can find something to be grateful for if they look for it. If you are among the few that can't find anything, start with the fact that you are ALIVE and continue from there. Counting ones blessings is a barometer of mental health. So stop for a moment and ask yourself, "What can I be truly grateful for at this very moment?" and reflect on the answers. Author and speaker Keith Cunningham recommends that we write down 200 things we are grateful for and then divide those 200 and place them on 10 to 20 index cards. He then recommends we carry those index cards around with us and read the things we are grateful for from time to time. He says this will give us a feeling of wealth and abundance – and I agree.

10. Do something everyday

If you wish to further increase your feeling of security, you can do so by adding one practice to your habitual life every week and/or every month. It may be saving money, cultivating better health, connecting with nature, finding ways to improve life through the use of science and technology or anything else you can think of.

Questions to help you grow

· What do I need to feel secure in all areas of life?
· How much money is enough (do the math and put down a number)?
· How can I further improve my health?
· How long do I want to live for (think about it)?
· Why do I want to live?
· What kind of things can I do to increase my vitality?
· What kind of shelter would I like to provide for me and my family?
· How much food is enough?
· How secure is my present social status?
· What would I like my social status to be in the future?
· How am I contributing to social cohesion (through politics, social structure, material structure, morals, community work, philosophy, etc.)?
· What am I doing to make this planet a safer place for myself, my family and humanity at large?
· How can I use science to improve my life?
· In the case of my death, is my family securely provided for?

... and last but not least:
· Is there any way to be totally and absolutely secure?

Affirmations

· I create my own security!
· I save and invest money to build financial security.
· I am confident about my own earning ability.
· I exercise regularly, watch my diet, relax, breathe deeply and think positively to take good care of my health.

· I work for social cohesion to ensure my own safety and that of my family and friends.
· I find constructive ways to use scientific knowledge .
· My daily actions show a commitment to mutual balance and harmony between humanity and the environment.

The 2nd Need

The Need for Excitement and Creativity

"Human nature, if it is healthy, demands excitement;
and if it does not obtain its thrilling excitement in the right way,
it will seek it in the wrong. God never makes bloodless stoics;
He makes no passionless saints."
- Oswald Chambers

The second need is so closely related to the human sex drive that it could be called the need for procreation or the need for sexual expression or sensuality. A person cannot participate in sex without getting excited and aroused and the human race would not exist without sex; so it is the ultimate creativity to participate in the creation of another human being. The sex drive is basic, but the need for sensual stimulation can also be met through other forms of excitement and creativity in other areas of life. For example, a child without any knowledge of sexual energy will still have the need for creativity, excitement and sensual stimulation such as food, stroking, listening to music, creating, cuddling etc. People also get excited in relation to sports and achievement and use their creative energy in a variety of different ways. Therefore, I have decided not to link this need exclusively to sexual procreation, although sex is an undeniable part of every person's life and should not be repressed.

Everyone must have excitement in their life. But the excitement must include security because every need transcends but also includes the preceding need or needs. The whole entertainment industry is centered on this theme. In a movie theater people feel safe but the sights and sounds make them feel excited. During times of war and uncertainty, humans are more likely to opt for security and shy away from excitement, but in peaceful and secure times, the search for excitement abounds. All forms of sensual excitement and entertainment are a big part of our culture when we feel secure and can be the source of great stimulation and momentary pleasure. But the flames of sensual pleasure can never be extinguished by giving way to more sensual pleasure. How much chocolate can one eat? How many fancy meals can one have? How much sex can one indulge in? At some point or another, if excessively pursued, the once pleasurable sensation will cease to be pleasurable and start to create pain. If you indulge excessively in sensual pleasure it will slowly but surely deaden the senses and you will need more and more stimulation to create minimal pleasure or excitement.

The *Bhagavad-Gita* explains attachment to the senses in the following manner:

> *"Thinking about sense-objects*
> *Will attach you to sense-objects;*
> *Grow attached and you become addicted;*
> *Thwart your addiction, it turns to anger;*
> *Be angry, and you confuse your mind;*
> *Confuse your mind, your forget*

the lesson of experience;
Forget experience, you lose discrimination;
Lose discrimination, and you miss
life's only purpose."

It's the attachment to sense objects that creates bondage. Nothing is said about not having pleasure, so long as you're not attached to it. Balance or transcendence is recommended, not repression. Now I don't pretend to have transcended any of the primal needs, but I have been told what it looks like by my teachers. However, it must be emphasized that very few people have actually mastered the transcendental approach to life and it is only recommended for *serious* spiritual aspirants. Transcendence means using the sensual, sexual, exciting, procreating energy and channeling it in order to create greater vitality and higher levels of feeling and thinking. But transcendence is so rare that I much prefer using the term balance. Repression on the other hand is based on fear, and fear will not yield a balanced, happy or healthy life. If repressed the need for excitement can become a shadow element in your psyche, waiting for the appropriate (or in most cases inappropriate) moment to rear its ugly head. The misuse of sex, drugs, alcohol and other regressive or anti-social behavior can in many cases retrace its roots to an excessive pursuit or repression of this need. But, this is such a primal need that each human being must dedicate a part of his or her life in the pursuit of some sort of balance and discipline that is associated with harmony and health. You can use this energy to support you and drive you forward in everything you do, or you can just as easily become a slave to the senses and lose all control of your life. This is true of almost any sensory experience. Keeping the sense organs finely tuned through discipline is the most beneficial way to attain pleasure in the long run.

The creative aspect

"All children are artists.
The problem is how to remain an artist once one grows up."
- Pablo Picasso

Human beings are highly creative creatures. Working on the assumption that we are created in the image of God we must also assume that we have been given some of Gods attributes. The role of Creator is probably the most commonly applied to the image of God. If we were created in His image we must continue to create. That is one of our roles in life. Masters of all ages have noticed that if this creative energy can be balanced, transcended, disciplined and put to good use in other areas of life, almost anything can be achieved. But this is a big IF. It is one reason why so many spiritual seekers take monastic vows and swear to live celibate lives. Behind most monastic vows is the philosophy of transcendence, again meaning that this creative force can be used to further evolve on the spiritual path. Unfortunately and in too many cases, these vows end up taking the form of repression instead of transcendence. Almost everyone has heard of the sexual abuse cases related to Catholic priests, and I have read and heard about many spiritual masters from the East who have fallen prey to the underside of the sexual energy. Disciplining and transcending the creative and sexual (sometimes called *kundalini*) energy is no easy task and should not be undertaken lightly. It requires adequate cognitive understanding and the direction of a spiritual master who has undertaken the vow successfully (and they are few and far between, even though many claim to have mastered the elusive kundalini energy). Again, I have my doubts about transcendence, so I recommend the balanced approach for the majority of people.

Positive outlets

"Wake up with a smile and go after life....
Live it, enjoy it, taste it, smell it, feel it."
- Joe Knapp

Everyone needs to find positive, practical and secure outlets, ways of having excitement, pleasure and creativity in their life. This can be attained through a disciplined amount of food, exciting sexual encounters with a willing and committed partner, movies and all artistic expression such as music, theater, artifacts and all kinds of sports, to name a few avenues. Find a way to use excitement, this passionate energy, to enrich your life instead of letting it assume control. Find a way to make everything you do more fun. Sexual energy, procreation, excitement and pleasure can be the basis for some of life's richest moments.

For this need to have positive effects in your life you must learn to direct and discipline your creative energy. This can only be done through understanding and experimentation, not repression and dogmatic condemnation. Find a channel for this need, a way to excite yourself about life, find pleasure in the simple things, the mundane, the natural, find a way to use your creativity and commit to getting up every morning, full of energy, with a smile on you face and learn to live with passion.

My father overcame many of his difficulties in life through the method of having fun and being passionate. He was always laughing, singing and joking around to the immense joy of himself and the people around him. Although he experienced much physical pain for over thirty years due to sores on his feet, he never complained about them. Instead he always woke up with a smile, always ready to do something fun, something exciting. He found a way to use this need for excitement and creativity to overcome some of the hardships of life. At his funeral, over a thousand people showed up. His joy and excitement had touched so many people in the course of his life that they came in order to pay their last respects.

Out of Balance

As already discussed, many of the actions society deems as immoral and destructive stem from this need for excitement, sensual stimulation, pleasure, sex and creativity. It is precisely because this need is so hard to control that every person *must* and should give it consistent attention and learn ways to curb its negative effects. When dealing with this need everyone should remember to consider the darker side. Much of humanity's pain suffered from infidelity, drugs, alcoholism, tobacco, sexual abuse and overeating, to name a few, can be directly linked to this need. Having seen the ill effects an excessive pursuit of this need can have on human life, many institutions of power such as organized religions and governments have made up and enforced rules that are meant to repress the need and all energy linked to it. Anything vaguely resembling or symbolizing this exciting and creative energy has in many cases been deemed as sinful, bad, evil, from the devil and so on. Following these imposed rules many people have ended up rejecting a fundamental part of their own psyche.

Many great books, much of the world's most famous music and many great paintings have been created by an artist in a sexually heightened state. This energy is so powerful and so enticing that many artists have become slaves to excessive sensory gratification, and that in turn has led to the detriment of their other needs and their lives in general. Some of them have unleashed their creativity in such a way that they lose all control over their sensuality. They may have depth of heart and mind, but without any control over their senses some have become slaves and addicts to whatever their senses crave. This is not true of all artists, but it is certainly no secret that many great artists of all ages, have reached the highest levels of excess within their need for excitement and creativity.

Here are more examples of what the second need could look like if it were out of balance. Remember that out of balance means that the effects produced can have destructive or detrimental effects on the other needs discussed in this book.

Out of balance people are always looking for the next high at any cost. Some find a way to get excited by charging themselves up with negative emotions like anger and irritation. When their relationships seem dull they pick a fight. When their work is in a rut they get angry or frustrated. Any form of excitement will do. Other forms of excitement through sensual stimulation include listening to extremely violent and harsh music that invades the body and deadens the senses. Overeating is a popular way of finding secure excitement. Many people end up eating only for the sake of the taste buds and sensations, instead of eating for nutritional purposes.

The repression of this need for excitement can have equal or worse effects. Mental, emotional and physical instability can arise. A life without excitement can lead to boredom or in the worst-case scenario severe bouts of depression. This boredom can be brought about by feelings of guilt and repression. Repression can also explode and result in a temporary case of extreme expression, such as rape, molestation or any other form of aggression. Again I must emphasize, repressing is not balancing. Even though real spiritual masters have advocated the transcendence of these needs, they have been widely misunderstood and even misrepresented by their followers to the detriment of society.

Most people have some shadow elements within their psyche connected to their childhood or adolescence. But living in the shadows, afraid and ashamed is just as damaging as the uncontrollable pursuit of instant sensual gratification. It all comes down to the same thing. Master yourself! Find more harmony and some sort of balance. Balancing the need for excitement and creativity can be frustrating work, but any small advance made in this area can yield numerous extremely positive benefits.

Practical advice

1. Learn about the elements
Learn more about the elements of pleasure, excitement and creativity in your life through contemplation and introspection. Identify and eradicate destructive ways of fulfilling the second need. Books recommended in the resource category at the end of this book can help you do this, however, the most effective way is often to get involved in some kind of therapy because the shadow elements caused by repression, excessive expression or emotional trauma are often deeply buried and do not surface willingly.

2. Find a positive approach to sexuality
Learn about or find an approach to sexuality that has the most benefits for you. Would you like to maximize your pleasure and minimize the pain connected to sexual energy? Would you like to learn a spiritual approach to sexuality?

Learn how it is possible to use sexual energy constructively through reading books and attending courses. If you want to become celibate, be sure you are doing so because you have reached an understanding that if sexual energy is directed toward higher realms, divine bliss can be found there. But do not undertake vows of celibacy as a means of escape or repression, based on fear and worry, for that seldom leads to the desired outcome.

3. Work to control the senses
Learn the practice of sense control – first sensitize and discipline, then balance – don't deaden the senses through excessive indulgence. In yoga this practice is called *pratyahara*. If you do not want to go to great lengths in this area you can at least learn how to delay sensual gratification. Instant gratification has become a way of life in the Western world. Learning to delay gratification can actually increase your pleasure in the long run.

4. Have fun! Be childlike!
Talk to a child and ask them what they like to do. You will find that the list is endless if the child is relatively healthy, and kids get excited about the most mundane things.

So here is the question: What do you get excited about? What do you do to have fun? Many people become so serious after they reach their twenties and thirties that the only way they know of having fun is excessive indulgence in sensory gratification (drinking, drugs, sex, eating, etc.). There is much difference between what I call childish and childlike conduct. I am not recommending childish behavior that is totally selfish and immature. Childish people throw tantrums when everything isn't going their way. I am actually recommending the opposite. To find inspiration and awe in everything. My three-year-old son is my greatest teacher in this area. He approaches everything like it's a game, always having fun. Being childlike means finding more ways to have fun during the day, looking at the most mundane things and being excited about them. In essence it's about looking at the world through fresh and curious eyes.

5. Be creative

Stay alert and find constructive avenues for your creative energy. You don't have to be an artist but why not try painting, playing an instrument, singing, chanting, sculpting, sewing, knitting or any other form of creative endeavor. You have tremendous creative capabilities within you just like everyone else. If you don't direct them into constructive channels they will most likely find negative outlets - you might even start to *create problems* in your life (it's been known to have happened). Creativity is your birthright. Use it constructively!

6. Curb your need for speed

If you are always looking for new ways to get excited you will slowly but surely desensitize yourself and that will only result in a continued search for new highs; in essence you will find yourself trying something more extreme, more outrageous and even more dangerous all the time. Many people have let their need for speed get way out of hand, to the detriment of other needs and even to their own destruction. Don't let that happen to you.

7. Learn about the polarity between male and female energies

Learn to respect and use the polarity between male and female energies. This advice can be applied to all the needs, but it especially refers to the second need (for excitement and creativity), because of the sexual connection, and to the fourth need (for love and relationships). Research has shown that there is a substantial chemical difference between the male and female bodies that can explain many of their major differences in behavior. However, there is also an energetic component, a play between opposing male and female energies. In learning about the philosophy of *tantra* this difference becomes very clear. The biological and energetic differences can be the source of much quarrel and misunderstanding. If men and women want to learn to live in harmony they must learn to understand each other. If you want to further pursue this matter you will find resources at the end of this book.

Questions to help you grow

· What excites me?
· What are some of the positive and constructive ways for me to gain pleasure and sensual gratification?
· How can I learn to direct and balance sensual energy instead of repressing it?
· How can I further get in touch with this need without it having a damaging effect on other needs?
· How can I use my creative energy constructively?
· What can I do to discipline and direct this need without repressing it?

Affirmations

· I find pleasure and excitement in the simple things of everyday life.
· I practice safe and exciting sex with a consensual and committed partner.
· I realize that creativity, pleasure and excitement are things I need in my life and I give them proportionate attention, but at the same time I stay aware so I don't get lost in their seductive energy.
· I discipline my senses and direct my creative energy through constructive avenues.

Resolving the Contradiction between the 1st and 2nd Needs

"Experience keeps a dear school,
but fools will learn in no other."
– Benjamin Franklin

There is an apparent contradiction between the needs for security and excitement. If this contradiction is not resolved it can become the source of much inner turmoil. I will give you some examples from my own life. I used to pursue the need for excitement and creativity excessively by sleeping around, drinking alcohol, smoking tobacco and occasionally using drugs. I was in a rock and roll band and I thought I was a real bad boy. I even have the tattoos to prove it. After I told Yogi Hari my story at his ashram, he joked around when he was introducing me and said: "He used to be Bad-John, but now he is Good-John." (It's a pun on the pronunciation of my name Gudjon – and if you ever meet me, I'll probably use it to get you to pronounce my name correctly). Anyway, early into my twenties I realized that this kind of behavior was having an extremely negative effect on my life and my physical condition. I was underweight, stiff and out of control in many ways. I was promiscuous, cheating every time I got the chance and that in turn had the effect that none of my relationships lasted very long. My behavior came to a point where it really started affecting my work and health. That shook my foundations. I was violating my needs for security and love through an excessive pursuit of excitement. As a result, I eventually quit smoking, drinking and doing drugs. My sexual promiscuity came to an end and I settled down and got married. Through my effort to control this need for excitement, my life soon became very secure, but it also became very dull. When I realized that I had thrown the baby out with the bathwater I started experimenting with ways of pursuing the need for excitement without violating the other needs. I realized that if I would continue to repress this energy, it would eventually explode in my face. I had seen this happen in other people's lives and did not want to follow in their footsteps. This continual balancing act between security and excitement is a process that has been going well for me so far. I have trained myself to find pleasure and excitement in simpler things without having to use as much external stimulation. I play two instruments, the guitar and the harmonium, I sing, I like to dance, I play with my kids and joke around with my wife and friends. I watch TV and go to the movies. I like all kinds of sports and I try to find ways to turn everything I do into a game. I also find joy and excitement through my work and meeting interesting people. I'm having fun most of the time.

In order for you to live a balanced and harmonious life, you must find a resolution between these two primal needs. Find some form of security in all your efforts to pursue this need for excitement and creativity and vice versa. By uniting these two forces you will find more joy and peace in your life. But it doesn't end there – read on and learn more about the other needs you can include in your awareness.

The 3rd Need
The Need for Individual Strength

*"Low self-esteem is like driving through life
with your hand-break on."*
- Maxwell Maltz

Our thoughts, words and actions are the only things we can strive to control in life, and even that can take years of training. All other things are out of our control. We can influence them, yes, but we can't control them. Yet so many people spend much of their lives trying to control other people and circumstances, never really learning to control themselves at all. They don't understand that gaining individual strength, self-control, self-esteem, self-confidence and self-mastery - is probably the only way to influence the outside world. Philosophers, spiritual masters and inspirational speakers have echoed this thought throughout history; change yourself, then change your world.

The need for individual strength is within all of us. We want to feel in control and we want to feel that we are special. Regaining control over our life means assuming total responsibility for our thoughts, words and actions. It's as simple as that.

It stands to reason that cultivating individual strength actually means assuming control over oneself. Such control calls for *discipline*, the master skill of all achievers in life. Discipline can be defined like this: You do *what* you decide to do, *when* you decide to do it, *whether* you *feel* like it or not. Most people don't hold themselves to this kind of standard. It is, however, a common practice in yoga to start developing discipline as early as possible to curb selfish and slothful tendencies. Yogi Hari tells a story of when he started to meditate. He woke up early every morning but nearly fell a sleep every time he tried to meditate. As a solution he tied a string to the ceiling and then tied it to his hair so that every time he was about to doze off the string would pull his hair and wake him up. He could then again concentrate on his meditation practice. I'm glad to say that he doesn't meditate with a string tied to his hair now. It was a temporary means to an end, a drastic measure but it worked. But here is my question for you: When it comes to discipline, how committed are you when you decide to do something? Do you follow through or do you make up excuses?

It's who you become

"A goal is a dream with a deadline."
- Napoleon Hill

Because goal setting and individual strength are so interrelated, I would like to share a few ideas on the art of goal setting and finding a major definite purpose in life. In his audio program *Lead the Field*, Earl Nightingale defines success as "the *progressive realization* of a worthy ideal or goal." I have done my share of writing down, pursuing and achieving goals and I must stress that Nightingale's definition is absolutely right; it's all about the *journey*, not the destination. It's having a dream when you wake up in the morning, having a purpose in life. Dr. John Eliot quotes a research done on centenarians (people who live to be a 100) in his audio program *The Maverick Mindset*. The research shows that there are only two commonalities found within their *lifestyle* to explain why people have become so old (the third reason is genes), and they weren't what the researchers were expecting. One thing they all had in common was regular exercise. That wasn't too surprising, but the other factor was a surprise. The researchers described factor number two as a *sense of purpose*. The people who lived to be a hundred had something to live for! So ask the question and reflect on it: "What do I have to live for?"

The energy that comes from individual strength and identity is more enduring and sustainable than the sexually charged and possibly volatile energy related to the second human need. It is closely related to the energy of the nervous system, especially to the bundle of nerves situated in the center of the body just below the ribcage and diaphragm referred to as the solar plexus. In yogic terms this energy is called *prana* but in English it is often referred to as the life force. Our whole being is made up of energy. If we learn to build and manipulate this energy we will find ourselves in a healthy and vibrant state every day.

Here are a few words on the subject of individual strength by my teacher and friend Yogi Shanti Desai taken from his new book, *Personal to Global Transformation*:

"Psychologists recommend building ego while spiritual masters recommend dissolving the ego. One needs to build ego before he can dissolve it. Building ego means building self confidence, assertiveness and will power. Without ego, one cannot exist or

succeed in life. One needs to wake up early, practice yoga, follow
spiritual disciplines and face challenges in life. One can use ego to
rise above ego. Venom medicine is made from the venom itself to
fight the poison of a snake bite."

This is yet another example of the seeming contradictions of an integral approach to life. Before giving up the ego or individual strength, one must build it and use it as a stepping stone towards further growth. Humility is the other side of the coin and in reality it is the full realization of individual strength and closely related to the fourth need of love as Yogi Shanti Desai goes on to explain:

"Humility is the climax of strength and wisdom. It is not weakness.
Fruit laden trees bow down. Humility is generally misunderstood
by society. Christ taught that if one slaps you on the cheek, hold
the other cheek. This compassion is the act of a brave person. One
has to build enough strength to strike back before holding the other
cheek. Maturity of strength produces humility. One can cultivate
humility by using affirmation, prayer, meditation, introspection
or surrender. Surrender does not mean defeat but attunement.
Surrender to God means being humble to receive divine qualities."

Out of Balance

Having a small, selfish ego, fighting, comparing and competing is the mark of imbalance in relation to the need for individual strength. This imbalance can take many forms. It's the basic power struggle that contaminates and infiltrates many marriages, friendships, corporations, governments and societies. Anywhere you find individual strength out of balance you will find phrases like: "I must have respect." - "Don't insult me." -

"I'm right, you're wrong." - "I'm better than ...." - "My (whatever) is better than yours." – the list goes on and on. It is the reason for many divorces, religious quarrels, political battles and even all out wars between nations. This is why the need for individual strength must be countered with the cultivation of humility and is also a good reason for having a set of moral principals to live by. In relation to the seven human needs it would be immoral to pursue or fulfill one need while violating another. There is no freedom without discipline. Undisciplined freedom will lead to chaos. Those who advocate total freedom without restrictions have clearly not acquainted themselves with the hierarchical growth of developmental psychology, ranging from selfish to care to world care. A child that gets no discipline while growing up becomes a selfish monster. The first thing any society must do to rise out of social chaos is to establish discipline, order and control. The same is true with increased individual strength. Growing from selfish to care to universal care requires a disciplined framework. Controlling selfish desires and tendencies requires the same kind of discipline that a child should have in his or her upbringing.

Of course there are a few more downsides, some of which discourage people from actively pursuing individual strength in the first place. People use phrases like "power corrupts and absolute power corrupts absolutely" to get out of the practice of pursuing self-confidence and self-esteem. People say something like: "Oh, I don't want to be stuck up, thinking I'm better than everybody else." You need to remember that the need for individual strength can sometimes be misinterpreted as the need for power over others. This is not the reality however. The need to exercise power over others or be better than everyone else stems from low self-worth and low self-esteem rather than individual strength. A true leader is a visionary and servant of the people, not a tyrannical dictator who oppresses and mistreats. Be aware that a very positive original intent can be subverted into a power struggle through politics if the person gaining power over others has not yet gained power over him/her self (politics is used here in the most general sense - office politics for example). Finding true self-worth and individual strength often means that you have to explore all the parts of your own being to find any restraints or shadow elements that might be holding you back. Past events imprinted in the subconscious mind might be the handbrake that an otherwise strong person may be held back by. It is said that self-analysis is best done with another person because of the mirroring effect. In the Western world we have many different methods that proclaim to be able to change subconscious imprints. Most people can find some benefit through using one or more of these methods to become aware and eradicate any restraints holding them back from finding true individual strength.

Problems that stem from low self-worth are too numerous to count. It may be the worst disease that has ever afflicted human kind for the following reason (among others): If a person with low self-esteem practices the golden rule of "love thy neighbor as thy self" the consequences can be disastrous. If I do not love myself, how can I love my neighbor? And how will I treat my neighbor if I have low self-esteem? The answer of a person with low self-esteem is: "Probably with the same or similar contempt and neglect that I treat myself with every day." You may protest and say that many people with seemingly low-self esteem spend much of their life giving to others. My answer to that comes in the form of a question: "Could a person give more and be of more service if he/she had high self-esteem and individual strength?"

Practical Advice

1. Learn how to influence and control your internal dialogue

Controlling your internal dialogue is mostly centered on the idea of asking the right *questions*. Almost everything you do in your mind revolves around asking and answering questions like: What does this mean? Where is this going? Is this going to mean pleasure or pain? To control the inner dialogue you must learn to control your internal questioning. The real question is: *Is my internal questioning hurting me or helping me?* You really want to learn to ask constructive and empowering questions like: What can I learn from this? How can I make this better and have fun doing it? How can I turn this around? What is good about this? ... and so on. For more on the power of questions refer to the resources at the end of this book, especially the work of Anthony Robbins.

2. Choose your friends wisely

Your peer group in life will have more effect on your behavior than almost anything else. Most people cherish relationships so much (see the fourth need) that they will change their behavior to meet the expectations of their peer group, even if it goes against their own nature. In yoga, the practitioner is encouraged to meet with similarly minded people regularly. This is called *satsang*. You will find a theory of this kind in all religions and communities, and almost all inspirational speakers stress this point on association. One quote I heard recently says: "You are the average of the five people you spend the most time with," (I heard this from Keith Cunningham but the original source is unknown to me). Choosing your friends is not an easy thing to do. You may have to limit relations to people you care deeply for because of their negative attitude towards life. But if you want to grow, evolve, inspire and be a positive uplifting human being, you *must choose* who you spend your time with.

3. Chart a course for your future

Have no destination and you will get lost. Charting a course for your life is extremely important. Much has been written on goal setting and many people have found the practice to be of much value. Working for something you believe in will give your life added importance. It will cause you to wake up with more energy, stay focused when chaos is surrounding you and help you keep a positive mental attitude when nothing seems to be going your way. And believe it or not, you will find it easier to live in the now, in the present moment. The reason is that if you know where you are going and you have charted a course that should get you there, you can plan your day and take a single step at a time in the right direction without always thinking about the final destination.

According to Brian Tracy there are no unrealistic goals, only unrealistic timetables. Most of the books and audio courses recommended in relation to the third need have to do with the process of charting a course for your future – the process of dreaming big dreams and setting the goals to achieve those dreams.

4. Find inner strength

If you rely on the environment for praise and strength you will not get very far in life and probably run into continuous disappointment. It is better to take charge of your own life and learn to rely on yourself. Trust your inner strength, because you have so much more of it than you realize. It is only when you give away your power and start relying on the outside world to provide for all your needs that you start losing your individual strength. Many people link their idea of self-esteem to material objects or situations. They end up thinking they are only noteworthy or valuable if they have enough money, drive the right kind of car, associate with the in-crowd, have the right body shape or are constantly told they are doing good, are beautiful or something along those lines. The source of your strength must be *internal* for individual strength to last. Otherwise you become a pawn in the chess game of life. According to Dr. John Eliot self-confidence is the sum total of all the thoughts you have about yourself. *What's the sum total of your thoughts?*

5. Be a student – not a follower

This is a crucial point for everyone interested in progressive self development and should be *related to all the human needs.* Yogi Shanti Desai taught me the six steps every student must take. They are: Learn, digest, apply, benefit, share and serve. Many people jump straight from learning to sharing. The reason is that they have become followers instead of being students. Not taking the time to digest, apply and benefit, the follower subscribes to a dogma in whole or in part and starts teaching it without any personal reference or experience. The student on the other hand approaches any situation with an open mind. He listens to the teaching or argument, asks questions and digests the information to see if it makes sense to him. He then applies the teaching with diligence and as a result he gains first hand knowledge of the perceived benefits. The student is then ready to share and serve others with the knowledge and wisdom gained in the process.

6. Learn to manipulate your body chemistry through posture

When I started doing yoga *asana* (physical postures) I was pleasantly surprised to find the following effects: While I was learning to breathe deeply and keep my back straight I found a rise in my self-esteem and self-confidence. Since then I have learned more about the effect of posture on the mind. The effect of body chemistry on the psychological state of a human being is rather amazing. Study after study has shown a close relation between regular exercise and good mental health. This relationship between body chemistry and the mental state can be taken a step further by realizing that anyone can change their body chemistry in an instant by changing their posture and breathing. A radical change in body chemistry can result in a radical change in mental state. This can be used to gain both positive and negative results. For example, the universal posture for depression and sadness is slumped shoulders, head down and shallow and irregular breathing. On the other hand you find that the universal posture for a positive mental attitude is a straight back, lifted head, shoulders back and deep breathing. Although posture is not the only means for a change of state, the powerful link between the two should not be overlooked. Mastering change of state through posture and mental focus should be the goal of anyone concerned with growth and balance in life.

Questions to Help You Grow

· What do I need to believe to feel confident about myself?
· How can I increase my self-esteem?
· How can I further increase my vitality?
· What is my main purpose in life?
· How can I further increase my individual strength and at the same time avoid narcissistic tendencies?
· What can I do to cultivate humility?
· How would I define individual strength?

Affirmations

· I am responsible for my thoughts, words and actions.

· I am a confident human being.

· I control my inner dialogue.

· I use my body to feel positive and powerful.

· I have a clear vision of my future.

· I am a work in progress – I can always find ways to become better and better.

· I use my self-esteem to benefit other people.

· I am strong but humble.

· I am becoming the change I want to see happen in the world.

The 4th Need

The Need for Love and Relationships

"Only love can change the world.
No systems, from left or right,
can bring peace and happiness in the world."
- J. Krishnamurti

Love equals relationships. To experience love you must be in a relationship, with yourself, your lover, your spouse, your children, your friends, your family, nature, the universe or your creator, to name a few of the most common love relationships. Love has been named the glue that holds people together. Some even say that it holds the universe together. A child that receives no touch and no love when newly born can actually whither away and die. Love is the most spoken about, written about, sung about and expressed feeling in the world. But anyone speaking of love must realize that there are many types of love. There is the excitement at the beginning of a relationship (closely related to the second human need for excitement and sex), a mother's love for her child, the love of a married couple, the love for a friend, the master's love for his student, God's love for His children and so on.

Three types of love

"For every beauty there is an eye somewhere to see it.
For every truth there is an ear somewhere to hear it.
For every love there is a heart somewhere to receive it."
- Ivan Panin

For the purpose of clarification I will now describe three distinct types of love. First there is the vividly expressed romantic love, often based on selfish desires, wants and needs. Second is the ethnic love for a family, spouse or nation, where a person's love is confined to the group the person relates to. Within a personal relationship it could also be called *"a give to get"* kind of love. The third kind is a mature and often spiritual kind of love, in which a person gives of his/her time and energy, with no expectation of return, to help another person grow and mature to reach higher potential. In a personal relationship this is called *unconditional love*. In larger context this third kind of love can also be an example of selfless service for the benefit of mankind. It is closely related to the need for a spiritual connection and can often be seen in the actions of spiritual masters. Recent examples include Gandhi, Mother Teresa, Nelson Mandela, the Peace Pilgrim, the Dalai Lama and a few others.

These distinctions seem to correlate with scientific findings. According to research in developmental psychology, there is a definite growth pattern of at least three (or more) stages which are closely related to the three kinds of love. I have touched on them briefly before. These stages of moral development are called selfish, care and universal care. The goal of anyone working for love and world peace should at least be to grow to the stage of universal care. Only through personal growth can there be a possibility for world peace and therefore each individual must to his/her part. Developmental psychology states that hierarchical growth is a stage conception that means you become more inclusive in your worldview as you evolve, more compassionate, sympathetic and caring – less narcissistic and selfish. This involves moral development. In my opinion there are a few reasons for the use of moral principals and moral virtues. One reason is that moral principals should be upheld for the sake of social cohesion. This point of view is closely related to the need for security, law and discipline. Social cohesion is based on how well people get along with each other, how they feel about each other, interact, etc., so it is closely interconnected with this fourth need. Another reason for morality is the curbing of volatile and animalistic tendencies that human beings have shown throughout history. These tendencies are mostly found within the framework of the first three needs, so when people fear for their security, are sexually aroused or are fighting for power, they tend to become animalistic in their behavior. History shows that because of the first two reasons morality has been imposed on humanity through religion and governments as a set of rules, laws and regulations. The basic human right is the freedom to pursue anything so long as it does not harm another person. The bottom line is that no one should be allowed to inflict harm upon others while in this animalistic state, hence the laws. But even though people follow the rules it remains a fact that moral development cannot be forced upon one human being by another. That brings us to the third reason and in my opinion the best reason for living in line with a set of moral principles. The third reason is ones own inner dialogue and corresponding relationships. Following a set of moral principles is the easiest and most productive way to find peace of mind, inner harmony and balance and that in turn brings corresponding outer balance. Your relationships are a reflection of your inner emotional state. The practice of adhering to moral principals creates balance between thoughts, words and actions. Inner turmoil created by animalistic tendencies and social struggle is soothed and energy clan be directed into more constructive avenues. Moral principles can be found in all of the worlds religions and they are the basis for an integral yoga practice, but moral disciplines should first and foremost be followed because of *understanding*, not as imposed rules and regulations, or because we want to please another (God, priest, family). A good guideline for inner balance is harmonizing the seven human needs. When you excessively pursue one need and violate another in that same endeavor, you are behaving immorally towards yourself. I have touched upon this theme in the chapters on the second and third need, precisely because they are interrelated. Each successive need includes some components of the previous needs, so the pinnacle, the need for spiritual connection includes all the previous components. But let us for now focus on the need for love.

Forgiveness

"To err is human, to forgive divine."
- Alexander Pope

In order to love others, you must learn to love yourself. A light bulb will not shine for others unless it can illuminate itself first. This kind of self love includes the practice of forgiveness. You must forgive yourself and others. I have read much about forgiveness and even written about it in my previous books and I have come to the conclusion that the act of forgiveness is in essence the most *selfish* act anyone can undertake. Yes! Forgiveness is selfish for the following reason. Any hatred or negative emotion directed at another person or at oneself, usually only ends up hurting the person who harbors the negative emotion. The person who is hated usually doesn't feel a thing, but hatred consumes the person that hates and can even be the cause of physical, mental and emotional distress and disease. Forgiveness is not equal to acceptance or condolence. Forgiveness only lets you off the hook, not the perpetrator; it gives you freedom from hatred, irritation and other negative emotions.

Learn to love yourself, forgive yourself and be kind to yourself. Then it must follow, as the day follows the night that you will start to love others. Practice the art of expanding this love from the inside out. Love yourself and then start expanding your heart and mind to include others. Start with your family, your friends, your co-workers, then expand to your community, your society, your country, keep expanding to neighboring countries and then include the whole world. Very few people ever get to this stage of loving the whole world, usually because they start by trying to love others first without having a firm grounding in self-love (not to be confused with selfish-love). Indeed, when a person comes to the point of loving his or her community, country and people of other faiths, nationalities and creeds, he/she starts appearing very spiritual.

Many never find love because they are afraid and unable to give love. Most relationships entered into willingly can be said to be a reflection of the emotional state of both persons in the relationship. Be sure you come into all your relationships as full of love and self respect as possible and focus on giving and expanding the feelings you already have.

Magnifiers of human emotion

"Relationship... is the mirror in which you discover yourself.
Without relationship you are not;
to be is to be related;
to be related is existence.
You exist only in relationship;
otherwise you do not exist;
existence has no meaning."
- J. Krishnamurti

Relationships are extremely important to all human beings, because they serve as magnifiers for human emotion. Have you ever been alone and seen something wonderful and wished you had someone to share it with? People come together to celebrate, to grieve and to otherwise kindle the flames of human emotion. All spiritual masters have spoken about the power of association. Associate with the kind of people you want to be like.

Some people settle for relationships that are dull or even destructive and never experience the real emotion of love. They opt for security or some form of sensual gratification. If you want to love, surround yourself with loving people. A mother's love for her child is programmed into her body's chemistry. A healthy mother will manufacture the hormone oxytosin that helps her create a strong bond to her newborn child. Most people receive this unconditional love in the first stage of life and look for it through relationships with other people for the rest of their lives. The starting point in adult life is to *fill yourself with love* and then you will find love everywhere. Another person's love will never satisfy you if you do not love and respect yourself. But if you love yourself, their presence will magnify a love that is already present within.

Out of Balance

Many destructive emotions can be said to be the antithesis to love. Hatred, anger, greed, jealousy, envy, irritation and so on. But most of them can be put under the heading of fear. Fear and love cannot co-exist in harmony. Learning to look fear in the eye and do the thing you fear anyway is one of the most important skills you can acquire in life.

It's not really difficult to see where people are out of balance in this area. One extreme is people who alienate themselves from all kinds of relationships. The other extreme is when people loose their identity in a relationship. A person with more female energy is more inclined to do the latter. Some call it co-dependency or enmeshment. Both extremes are commonly due to lack of self-love and self-worth. It can be said that the foundation to relationships is built by pursuing the third need of individual strength. Many people lower their standards and stay in a loveless relationship even though they intellectually know better. They settle for an average relationship though they are really searching for love.

Practical advice

1. Love your Self!

It all comes down to the same thing. You must learn to love your true Self, your divine nature and your essence, not your mere ego or animalistic tendencies (instead, their acts must be forgiven and disciplined). This kind of Self love will translate into a love emanating from you to all other beings. Contemplate this thought: Love is the gentle balance between always *wanting to grow and expand* and realizing that you are *perfect just the way you are.*

2. Cultivate Your Relationships

Any relationship that is to improve with time must be cultivated. In his book *A Path with Heart* Buddhist monk and psychologist Jack Kornfield explains that the question facing most people on their deathbed is: "Did I love well?" However, the fear of rejection holds many people back from cultivating their relationships to a degree that would make them totally fulfilled. Don't let this happen to you. Take a chance and make a real commitment to the relationships you are in today, whether they are with your spouse, your kids, your family or friends. Commit to give of your time and energy, not only to sustain, but to further improve those relationships. You deserve love and loving relationships, but you must put in the work, the thought and the time needed for love to flourish in your life. Brian Tracy puts it this way: "Children and spouses spell love in the same way: T-I-M-E." Give the ones you love the *time they need* to spend with you. It's one of the best investments you can ever make.

3. Forgive

When I had the good fortune of translating Gerald Jampolsky's book *Forgiveness: The Greatest Healer of All* from English to Icelandic, I learned a lesson I will carry with me for the rest of my life. When I had completed the task I made a vow to always be willing to forgive, no matter what happened in my life. This has not been an easy task, but I am glad to say that I have kept my word so far. The rewards I have reaped are greater than any words can describe. I am a free man because of the simple act of forgiveness. I urge you to read Jampolsky's book and to open your mind to the possibility of forgiving everyone (including yourself) for everything that has ever happened that made you feel sad, angry, jealous or hateful. When I read stories about Jews forgiving the Nazis for the atrocities committed in the Second

World War and about rape victims forgiving their perpetrators, I realized that forgiveness is not about making the act right or the person committing the act right, it is about freeing yourself from the limitations of spiteful emotions that only end up hurting you, the one who harbors them. According to the Buddha, holding on to anger is like grasping a hot coal with the intent of throwing it at someone else; you are the only one who gets burned.

4. Learn about human development
Get interested; learn more about all forms of human development and you will acquire a deeper understanding of the human psyche. Armed with empathy you will be able to relate to more and more people in the world. Everyone has a reason for doing what they do. Discover some of the reasons through different models of development. I recommend various sources. For example; *Spiral Dynamics* by Beck and Cowan, M. Scott Peck's model of spiritual development found in his book *Further Along the Road Less Traveled*, Ken Wilber's integral philosophy summarized in the book *The Theory of Everything*, the six emotional needs which are the foundation of much of the work by Anthony Robbins, Howard Gardner's multiple intelligence model, Daniel Goleman's emotional intelligence and the list could go on. Learning about the seven human needs is one step in the right direction but I encourage you to learn more.

Questions to help you grow
· How can I love myself more?
· Do I need to forgive anyone (myself perhaps)?
· Do I enter a relationship to give or to get?
· Am I fully committed to all my relationships (to my spouse, children, family and friends etc.)?

- What can I do now to improve my current relationships?
- Do I spend enough time with the people I love?
- What makes me feel loved?
- How do I make other people feel loved?

Affirmations

- I love myself.
- I cultivate love in all my relationships.
- I am slow to anger – quick to forgive.
- I give love.
- My essence is pure love.

Resolving the Contradiction between the 3rd and 4th Needs

"Courage is resistance to fear, mastery of fear –
not absense of fear."
- Mark Twain

Wanting to be special, autonomous, distinguished and powerful can often clash with the need for love. When looking at the primal or basic four needs, one finds a very acute difference between male and female energies. Most of the time men have more male energy and women more female, although that is not always the case, since both men and women have a balance of male and female energies. In the ancient philosophy of tantra the male and female energies are quite well distinguished. The female energy is closely related to the first and fourth needs, the need for security and the need for love, and the male energy is closely related to the second and third need, the need for sensual stimulation (sex) and the need for individual strength. If you look around you will find many corresponding examples, and you may even be able to realize whether a man or woman generates more male or female energy. The conflict between the need for individual strength and the need for love causes much of the disturbance in modern day relationships. It's not an easy task and all the worse if people have been "hurt in the past" and are therefore distrusting and fearful. Adults of the modern generation do not need a relationship like marriage in the same way former generations did. A single person can fulfill all the needs for security, sensual stimulation and individual strength without committing to another person. It can even be said that the modern emphasis on individual strength through goal setting, unleashing inner power and other practices of today's society may in some cases have alienated love, long-term commitment, spirituality and other related ideas as relics of the past. Learning to live in a relationship for love's sake is a relatively new practice and many people may find that this is not as easy as it sounds. Marriages used to revolve around security and procreation, not love, although it was sometimes a healthy byproduct of the union. However the need for love is undeniable. In many cases pets have become substitutes for human love, because they do not make the same demands for growth and concession. I remember the words of a porn star I once read about. She said: "I go to my cats for love but when I want sex, I go to work." How crazy is that?

Learning to balance all the seven human needs with another person, be it a child, a friend or a spouse, is a commitment that helps you grow on a day-to day-basis. Being open to love means that you will most likely get hurt and you'll probably have to make some concessions in your need for individual strength. But don't let the need for love be suppressed for this reason. Face the fear and do it anyway. All relationships are a two-way street and should be treated as such.

Why is the first wave the foundation for the second wave?

"The only real voyage of discovery consists
not in seeking new landscapes but in having new eyes."
- Marcel Proust

I know it's obvious. It's like telling you that the number one comes before the number two. But the needs are in this order for a particular reason.

I have found many examples of people pursuing the second wave of needs (contribution, growth and spiritual connection) without having the first wave (security, excitement, individual strength and love) in balance - and this rarely, if ever, produces the desired results. However hard you look for it, and no matter what your religion tells you, what you have been raised to believe or what you want to believe, you will never find a tree that grows from the leaves down! Trees must grow from the roots up and in the same way we have to build firm foundations.

Now, let's look at an obvious example, i.e. the people who claim to be spiritual masters. Many cases in recent history have clearly shown that when a so-called spiritual master, that has proclaimed celibacy, humility and other seemingly spiritual traits, falls from his pedestal, it's usually related to a sexual scandal, a power struggle or the accumulation of money at the expense of his/her disciples. Many of the so-called Eastern spiritual masters have been brought up in a social background that suppresses the first wave of needs, especially the first (survival and security), second (sex and excitement) and third (individual strength). When they come to the West and are exposed to all kinds of temptations related to the first three needs, many of them find that they lack resistance and eventually fail in their effort to repress their primal needs. I liken this situation to learning to swim in the desert and then being thrown into the ocean and told to swim.

Real spirituality is the process of finding material and internal security (1st need), learning to enjoy life without deadening the senses (2nd need), finding individual strength (3rd need) and learning to love oneself and have loving relationships (4th need). These are the foundations of human life. Everyone must and will find ways, detrimental or healthy ways, to fulfill these needs. The second wave, consisting of contribution, growth and spiritual connection, relies on a relatively healthy foundation, built through fulfilling the first wave of needs in a constructive manner. It is precisely for this reason that most of the imbalance you find connected to the second wave, actually has its roots in the first wave. Some people think that the second wave is higher and therefore better than the first wave. Taking that point of view, many organized religions have advocated the repression of the first wave, but in order to stay healthy and whole each and every person must find a way to balance and pursue ALL these needs. That is the integral or holistic approach to life.

The second wave makes us distinctly human

"We either make ourselves miserable, or we make ourselves strong.
The amount of work is the same."
- Carlos Castaneda

To contradict myself, in a way, the religions are right. The second wave is more important because it makes us distinctly human. When the second wave is not met, a void will be felt within; a void that can't be filled by the pursuit of the first four needs (although many people try that first - and some even go through life without ever knowing about the second wave and its importance).

Observing the animal kingdom you will find examples of what people tend to think of as unique to human behavior - emotion, community and power struggles for instance. But when humans find corresponding behavior in animals it doesn't necessarily suggest that the animals are behaving in a human way, instead it may suggest that we humans are behaving in line with our original mammal and animalistic tendencies. In evolutionary terms all human beings still have some of the physical traits of preceding mammals, including a reptile brainstem and a horse brain. It's included in our physiology. Most mammals and many other animals seem to encompass the first three to four needs although they may not be expressed in exactly the same way as with us humans. All animals seem to have a drive to survive (security), a freely expressed and sexually active and procreative need (excitement and creativity), an order of importance, sometimes referred to as a pecking order (individual strength) and many of them have the ability to show emotion (love and relationships).

But only in humans do we find the three higher and often disregarded needs of contribution, wisdom and spirituality. Make no mistake. These are actual needs within every human being. If they are not fulfilled nothing else will fill the void. In civilized societies, where the first four needs have been met by most of the population, you will find generosity and contribution, a continuous search for wisdom and growth through science and academics and in many cases you will find highly developed spiritual masters (they need an affluent and peaceful society in most cases to be able to pursue the spiritual path). If a human being does not pursue the last three, he or she is missing a crucial part, the most human part. Let us now move on to the second wave of needs.

Why is the first wave the foundation for the second wave?

The Second Wave
of Needs

"We fear our highest possibility (as well as our lowest one).
We are generally afraid to become that
which we can glimpse in our most perfect moments."
- Abraham Maslow

The 5th Need

The Need for Expression and Contribution

"You can have brilliant ideas, but if you can't get them across, your ideas won't get you anywhere."
– Lee Iacocca

In the first seconds after every human birth, life is felt through a vibration in the vocal cords known as the first cry. The vocal cords are humanity's main tool for expression. Through our vocal cords we learn to express our likes and dislikes, our feelings, our thoughts, values and ideas. They are the medium of choice for most people. Our vocal cords express all the other human needs referred to in this book. But there are many other forms of expression, including the written word, art, body language, touch, smell and taste to name a few. All the senses can be used to express our internal monologue to create an external dialogue. Different modes of expression have different meanings for different people. Because of the varying meanings we put into different words and situations it can be rightly said that the most common form of understanding is *misunderstanding*. Many quarrels and even wars have started because of the inability of two or more persons to express their thoughts, feelings or social values in a way that makes them understood by others. Any person that wants to be understood should therefore make a great effort to exercise different modes of expression in a concise manner, especially the verbal, written and physical modes. Because of its necessity, extensive research has been done in the area of human communications. For those interested in exploring further ways to maximize the art of human expression, "tricks of the trade" can be learnt through courses and seminars. Successful salespeople, teachers and speakers seem to have trained these skills to a greater extent than most other people, probably because their security depends on it. But the sad fact is that many people fear public speaking more than they fear death. My opinion is that this fear should be overcome, or at least minimized, by everyone, not so that they can all make money through public speaking, but because there are so many instances in life where being able to stand up and speak one's mind is valuable. If you want to speak at your friends' funeral, voice your opinion in politics, congratulate your co-workers, get your ideas across to the CEO or speak at your child's wedding, the ability to express yourself verbally is likely to be a very precious skill. Anyone can learn the skill of expression if they take the time and effort to do the training necessary. Even if your only goal in life is to express spiritual truths - you must acquire this skill. All great spiritual masters have been good at getting their message across. In most organized religions you will also find the need for expression met through singing and chanting.

Beyond your limited self

"Giving connects two people, the giver and the receiver,
and this connection gives birth to a new sense of belonging."
- Deepak Chopra

Contribution is the ultimate form of expression. It involves expressing your values to the surrounding world. The need for contribution makes humanity special. Given the right circumstances and framework this need will arise in all human beings. There are great forces in the West and East dedicated to helping other people survive and thrive in the world. The very fact that people are willing to give of their time, money and energy to serve other human beings they hardly know is a staggering idea. This reflects a certain amount of emotional and spiritual well being. Most religions and spiritual paths recommend the practice of tithing, giving a part of all your earnings to those in need. In many parts of the world tithing has been legalized in the form of taxes, but that doesn't stop a large number of people from giving more of their time, money and energy to people in need. This is an expression of the similarities of mankind, of the human bond, of caring and of love. Contribution goes way beyond any one person. It has ties with moral, emotional, intellectual and spiritual values. The need for expression and contribution should transcend and include the previous needs in their healthy form.

Out of balance

The freedom of expression is the very foundation of most western societies. This right is held sacred, but it has been under attack in recent years. Through the global network now in place, many have started to use the freedom of speech to incite violence. The fundamentalist movements of many religions, often based in the need for security and individual strength (my faith is better than yours), have taken offense and protested many of the writings and pictures published in the West. There is no freedom without restraints, no freedom without discipline, but the freedom of expression is a sacred pillar of every free society. A global solution is not in sight at this moment, but every individual can do his or her best to find positive modes of expression, aimed at cohesion, not destruction. A critic, voicing opposition to unjust behavior, should be focusing on the correction of a problem and therefore his criticism should be constructive. The critic can offer solutions or at least ask for a debate about solutions. His task is not only to voice the problem.

An obvious deficiency in this area is a lack of expression. Many people have been criticized for their expression and communication from childhood onwards (maybe told to shut up a few too many times while they were growing up) and as a result they have started to repress their need for expression, instead of holding their head high and voicing their thoughts and opinions. Any form of repression can and most likely will create mental, emotional and even physical problems. So don't repress. In this respect it is good to think like a politician. Count the instances that work for you, not the ones that work against you. Every politician has a way of turning the numbers to his favor. This can be a very healthy practice if balanced.

The other side of the coin is excessive expression. An expression of every feeling, every thought and every criticism, just or unjust, should be tempered. Many people have taken this excessive expression and turned it into their primary mode of communication. They speak of every feeling, every like and dislike without regard of others, defending their actions with phrases like: "I'm only speaking my mind!" or "I'm only telling the truth." But always expressing your feelings and thoughts can go too far. And what is truth? Are your individual preferences, likes and dislikes a true reflection of some eternal truth? Of course not! Temper your expression. Author and speaker Brian Tracy says that one of the most liberating sentences anyone can utter is: "I could be wrong, I often am." I use it all the time, and he's right, it's truly liberating.

Freedom of expression should be coupled with discipline and respect. Only then can expression be of benefit to mankind. Only then can a person contribute freely and effectively. A wise choice of words should be the prime directive for all human relations. First think, then speak, then act!

As alluded to earlier it must be said that in order to contribute to the world you must first have a strong foundation. If you do not feel secure (1st need) you will not contribute but only hoard your "wealth" for yourself. If you do not discipline yourself and instead you constantly give in to sensual stimulation and sensual pleasure (2nd need) your money and time will only be spent on selfish activities. If you do not have self-esteem and self-respect (3rd need) you cannot see how your special gifts in this life can be utilized by the world around you. And if you do not have love (4th need) you will not see a reason to extend that feeling to other less fortunate people. It can therefore be said that any form of imbalance in this area is closely related to the imbalances found within the first four needs.

Practical advice

1. Learn about the different modes of expression

There are three major modes of communication and expression. They are visual (sight), auditory (sound) and kinesthetic (touch).

If you learn how to use these three modes and learn about your dominant mode of expression all your communications will become more effective. This will improve your listening skills and you will be able to hear, see and feel what the other person is saying and be able to respond in the same mode of expression, which will again greatly enhance the communication. To learn more read any book on NLP (Neuro Linguistic Programming) or type the keywords (visual, auditory, kinesthetic) into a search engine on the internet.

2. Take a course in public speaking
Having the ability to express your thoughts and feelings in public is probably on of the most important skills you can learn. Take time to do this even though it may scare the heck out of you. So many situations can come up in life where the ability to speak publicly can come in handy. You may have thought up a dozen instances already. If you don't want to learn public speaking, try taking an acting class or learn how to sing. Do what you can to train yourself. Your vocal cords are there for a reason. Use them!

3. Find out how you can contribute beyond your limited self
There are so many ways in which individuals can contribute beyond their own limited selves. Do some research. Check where the money goes if an institution asks for your charitable donation. Ask yourself the following questions:
· Do I want to contribute of my money, time or energy?
· What am I interested in?
· What am I good at?
· Where can I really contribute and make a difference?
Remember, if you give someone a fish today they will be hungry again tomorrow. Give someone a fishing rod and teach them

how to fish and they will become self-sufficient for a long time. In Indian society spiritual knowledge has traditionally been valued above everything else, but in essence, the poorest people in the world really need to learn to read and write so that they can further educate themselves.

Questions to help you grow

· What is my primary mode of expression?
· What can I do to refine, discipline and train
  my primary mode/s of expression?
· Can I express myself freely?
· Is my primary mode of expression repressed or excessive?
· What can I do to contribute beyond myself?
· What can I do to further improve myself in the area
  of expression and contribution?

Affirmations

· I express myself freely and openly.
· I could be wrong, I often am.
· I temper my expression with regard to others.
· I use my talents, knowledge and resources to be of service
  to society.
· I contribute beyond my limited self.

—

The 6th Need

The Need for Wisdom and Growth

"It is the mark of an educated mind
to be able to entertain a thought without accepting it."
– Aristotle

Knowledge is not power, even though most of our academic institutions advocate the opposite view. Knowledge is only potential power. Don't get me wrong. I have tremendous respect for academic institutions. They gather and preserve all human knowledge so that humanity may evolve and advance towards a brighter future. But many people seem to spend an enormous part of their lives acquiring information and knowledge that they never put to *good* use. It doesn't even enhance their own life, let alone the lives of anyone else in the world around them. It doesn't make any sense. To me, having the information and not acting on it, is plain stupid. I've been there myself many times. The fact is that only applied knowledge is power. Once someone applies the knowledge and reaps its rewards or punishments (action and reaction) the same someone slowly starts to acquire wisdom. Wisdom can be defined as the coupling of knowledge and experience, and in turn, that can lead to growth. It's all interconnected. Everything in nature is either growing or dying. The same is true of a human being. Life will either beat us to the ground or we will learn life's lessons, rise up and grow. All of life's experiences have a potential for advocating growth. But for the potential to ripen, the experiences must be met with a mindset of growth. Typical growth questions include: "What can I learn from this situation/person/state of mind?" "How can this help me grow?" "How can this painful experience be of benefit to me or others in the future?"

A willingness to grow doesn't necessarily make life any easier, but it does give life meaning, and according to Viktor Frankl - Holocaust survivor and author of the inspirational and breathtaking book *Man's Search for Meaning* - meaning promotes life. As a prisoner in the Nazi concentration camps of the Second World War he realized that some of his fellow prisoners found their life to have meaning, even amidst horrible circumstances. The ones who found meaning had a better chance of survival and, more importantly, found a way to contribute to their fellow prisoners. It's a story of triumph for the human spirit in circumstances where most people functioned only on basic survival instincts.

Contrary to popular belief, growth and wisdom do not necessarily come with age. In fact many people have been *infected* with what I call an anti-growth or anti-wisdom attitude. I use the word infected on purpose because this attitude can be a real disease driven by fear, anger and regret. Life's lessons can be hard and any person who has an anti-growth attitude can develop a hardening of the mind and become judgmental, fearful and bitter. It can sound something like this: "I should've, could've, if only I would've." "You don't know how hard my life has been." "You don't understand." "Life didn't give me a sweet deal." You get the picture. *Please don't let this happen to you.* The only difference between people who let life beat them down and the people that learn and grow from experience is *attitude.* Attitude is the wellspring. It determines how you interpret and therefore how you react to everything that happens to you.

Growth also comes from contemplating the knowledge already acquired, either by learning from others or learning through observation and experience. Dr. Albert Schweitzer was once asked what he thought was wrong with the world. He responded: "People don't THINK." Visionary and inspirational speaker Earl Nightingale, founder of the Nightingale-Conant Corporation, says that in his opinion many people go through the education system from beginning to end without ever learning to think for themselves. He says that memorizing like a parrot is not thinking, it is merely the retention of information. Albert Einstein concurred when he answered a question of how many yards there are in mile by saying that he didn't think it wise to fill his head with trivial information that he could easily find elsewhere if he needed to use it. Einstein's purpose was to think in an original way.

The most extraordinary tools for thinking available to mankind are *questions.* If you continuously ask and answer questions in your mind or on paper, then you are thinking. With a method taught by Earl Nightingale you can put this into practice.

- - - - - - - - - -

Start with a blank piece of paper. Write a question at the top of the paper about the most pressing matter that concerns your life today and discipline yourself to come up with at least twenty answers. The method is deceivingly simple and yet it is extraordinarily powerful. Try it a few times and see for yourself.

- - - - - - - - - -

If you are constantly growing, then you never become bored or taxed with weariness in life. Growth means that you are always expanding you horizon, always going beyond you comfort zone and you always retain the mental question: "What can I learn from this?"

Through intense thinking, contemplation and meditation you can receive flashes of intuition from time to time. This has happened to many scientists and spiritual masters through the years. For example much of yoga philosophy has been born through flashes of intuition. Isaac Newton had a flash of insight about gravity when an apple fell from a tree and hit him on his head and Albert Einstein had an intuitive insight about the theory of relativity when he was looking at a clock. Afterwards all of the above mentioned studied and researched their intuitive theories for a long time and put them through rigorous testing so that they could explain their original flashes of intuition to other people. Einstein tried this explanation for example:

"When a man sits with a pretty girl for an hour, it seems like a minute. But let him sit on a hot stove for a minute, and it's longer than any hour. That's relativity."

An intuitive flash is a thought or an idea that springs forth and is already fully formed. An intuitive flash can expand your horizon, by showing you that the mind is not merely confined to the boundaries of the brain. Many examples have been recorded of people in different parts of the world with no prior knowledge of each other and yet these people have had the same or similar flashes of insight within the same or similar timeframe. They have in essence gotten the same ideas at the same time. How can that be explained? Expand your mind and really think about that.

Let's turn back to the quest for knowledge for a moment. In this life you can acquire all sorts of useful knowledge. It should not be overlooked that you need practical knowledge about your surroundings, nutritional values, the financial and job market, health, evolution, science, philosophy, relationships, history, psychiatry, mathematics and the list goes on. It is best to say that there is still much to be learned. Worldly knowledge is progressing at rate never before known to mankind. To stay in the game of life, everyone must become a continuous learner. However it should be emphasized that practical knowledge will be of little use if you don't have Self-knowledge. The spiritual and philosophical traditions of the world have agreed that Self-knowledge is the highest form of knowledge. A person devoted to wisdom and growth will work ceaselessly to sharpen the intellect, train the mind and acquire Self-knowledge through practice and experience.

Out of Balance

The two extremes within this need are excessive knowledge and stupidity. Excessive knowledge can perhaps best be explained with this short story. It has been told many times in many books so you may have read it or heard it before, possibly in another version. The essence however remains the same, so here it goes.

A professor that had acquired great knowledge in his lifetime heard of a wise man in the mountains. The professor had an insatiable appetite to know everything there was to know in the world so he set out on an extremely hazardous journey to find the wise man. After traveling for an extended period of time, the professor finally came to his destination. The wise man told him to sit down and offered him some tea. Even though the professor was eager to learn, he decided to wait and accepted. The wise man then started to pour tea into the professor's cup. When the cup was full to the brim the wise man kept on pouring until the cup started overflowing. Still the wise man just kept on pouring. The professor protested: "What are you doing?" The wise man said: "Your cup is already full, I cannot teach you any more."

The story can be interpreted on many levels, but for the purposes of this book, the moral of the story is simple. When you are faced with a learning situation you must empty your cup, be humble and ready to receive knowledge. If you think you know, you will not learn anything. When the student is ready, the teacher appears. It's all about the *readiness* of the student. We have the possibility of learning from all sorts of teachers in our life; but in reality every circumstance we encounter can increase our skills and knowledge if we get into the mindset of a student.

What I call stupidity on the other hand is not only lack of knowledge, although much of humanity could be elevated from poverty, dogma, illusions and war through traditional education. A thriving education system is the foundation for progress. But stupidity is not merely ignorance; it can also be a way of acting. If you act contrary to your own goals in life – you're stupid. The wise of this world align thoughts, deeds and words to be coherent in everything they do. Many people act in a stupid manner even though they have information contrary to their actions. For example: A doctor who smokes cigarettes cannot be considered wise however knowledgeable he may be. Now think: Have you ever known better and acted to the contrary of your own knowledge? Of course you have – and so have I. To avoid this as much as you can in the future, try to make certain that your actions, thoughts and words are in line with the knowledge you already have and that they match your goals, dreams and visions in life. Remember, knowing is not the mere retention of information. Knowing is also doing!

Practical advice

1. Ask questions and contemplate
The method of asking questions is highly effective. You can ask questions of yourself and force your mind to come up with answers (as described earlier in this chapter) or you can associate with people that are smarter and wiser than you are and ask them questions. The only praise I have received from both of my yoga teachers through the years, has been the remark: "You ask very good questions." Of course this has not always been the case. Sometimes I ask stupid questions. But I have made the link in my mind that not asking questions is more painful than asking. Many people have it the other way around. They don't want to appear foolish so they never ask and therefore never gain the knowledge they desire. Once you receive answers, either from the depths of your own mind or from other sources, pause for a while and contemplate what the answers really mean. For example, if you are reading and a question comes to mind – stop and reflect on it. The mere act of contemplating and reflecting is overlooked by many people. You have much of the knowledge and wisdom already within

yourself; you only have to uncover it. Plato said that the most important knowledge is already within the student. He called himself a "midwife of recollection" – not a teacher.

2. Choose your mental diet carefully

Whatever goes into your mind has a reflection – and the reflection of your thoughts is called *your life*. In the words of the Buddha: "All that we are is the result of what we have thought. The mind is everything. What we think, we become."

Many people go to great lengths to keep their body healthy by choosing carefully what they eat. The same should be true about your mind and you should be very careful of what you put in there. Research has shown that a continuous intake of violent images for example, doesn't necessarily make a person more violent, but it desensitizes the person and makes all forms of violence more acceptable. Really pause and think about the consequences before you watch a movie, a television program, read a book or associate with other people. The power of thought is undeniable and becomes greater as the mind is strengthened through practice. I urge you to be aware and continually ask: "Is this really something I want to put into my mind?" If you have children try to pre-screen some of the material they are watching and ask: "Is this really something I want to allow into the mind of my kids?"

To further emphasize this point let me relate a story about a conversation I had with a principal a few years back that really stuck in my mind. When the conversation took place I was a guest at his school lecturing about smoking prevention. He came to me and said: "I'm not really worried about these kids smoking. We've had a smoke free school here for some years now. I am however worried about a large number of boys between the ages of ten and fifteen because all these kids do is play computer games after school. I see them become disinterested and bored with school and life in general. It's like an addiction, and as a result it seems they are living in a different reality. They act like they are serving prison time in school and are living their true identity through their computer games. I am worried about what their future will be like. I talk to the parents but they are busy. These kids are in a very dangerous situation." Recent news here in Iceland report that several young boys have been admitted into the mental ward of our hospital because of playing computer games for too long. I fear that we have only just begun to see the repercussions computer games can have on our young people and the society as a whole.

3. Read more

Reading has changed my life for the better. As you can see within the context of this book, I highly recommend reading any kind of material that you consider beneficial to your way of life; in essence, read anything that can expand your mind and help to keep your attitude positive and constructive. Strangely enough I didn't really get into the habit of regular reading until I quit smoking. After freeing up the time, I made a habit of carrying a book around with me everywhere I went and began reading whenever I got the chance. The moments were often short but I was pleasantly surprised to realize that reading for five to ten minutes, the same amount of time it took to smoke a cigarette, I could get through a couple of pages and that in turn meant quite a few pages every day. To make a long story short I have read hundreds of books as a result of this change of habit and my life is all the better for it. My lack of formal schooling has not hurt me as much as it could have because of my continual quest for self-knowledge.

4. Listen to audio programs

Another practice that has positively impacted my life is the habit of listening to audio programs in my car or when I go out for a walk. If you want to become a continuous learner, the act of listening to audio programs will greatly enhance your life. First I started listening to tapes, then I bought CD's and now I use my iPod constantly. Using this technology has greatly enhanced my life in all the areas discussed in this book and more. You can purchase audio programs about almost anything. My favorite websites for purchasing audio programs are: Nightingaleconant. com, Audible.com and Soundstrue.com. If you get in the habit of listening to audio programs you will never go back to merely listening to the radio.

5. Attend courses and seminars

Attending courses and seminars is like taking a book or an audio program to the next level. The presence of a teacher and the atmosphere created by a crowd outweighs the mere acts of reading and listening by far. You also meet people who are interested in the same things that you are interested in. I am committed to life-long learning and I attend at least two or three courses or seminars every year. I also keep a close relationship with my yoga teachers. I contact them regularly and make an effort to see them at least once or twice a year. This might not sound like a lot but if you consistently keep it up for a few years it will translate into some real results.

6. Try not to say: "I know."

This one has been, and still is, a hard one for me. Being a "know it all" is not very helpful when it comes to learning situations. Saying "I know," or "I've already heard this," when you are *not a living example* of the principals being taught, actually retards any learning situation. By thinking instead "Maybe I don't know this so well since I'm not doing it," can help you stay open minded and that in turn can facilitate the learning experience. My point is that if I think something will enhance my life, I keep reading about or listening to the same principals and even going to the same seminars, until the applied knowledge becomes my second nature, even though I've heard it or read about it many times before.

7. Get around people that are smarter and wiser than you are
In order to take this advice seriously it is very important that you are humble enough to realize that your sense of individual strength is not limited to your cognitive capacity. An inferiority complex can in many cases prevent people from associating with others that are smarter or wiser than they are. If you want to get better at anything (and that's a big IF) you must get around people who are your superiors. Playing a sport with someone who is better than you are means that you have to step up to the challenge and that in turn will increase your ability faster than almost any other practice. The same is true with cognitive ability. Reading something you barely understand or engaging in conversation with people that challenge you, will greatly enhance your cognitive abilities. Emerson put it this way when he depicted a true scholar: "In every man there is something wherein I may learn of him; and in that I am his pupil."

Questions to help you grow
· How can I keep on growing and expanding?
· How can I further train my cognitive ability?
· What do I like to read and learn?
· Am I willing to learn and grow?

- What is my motivation behind learning?
- Do I use what I know?
- Can I use more of what I already know? What and how?
- Am I willing to be a student for life?

Affirmations

- I am always learning and growing.
- I read material that positively impacts my life.
- I love to read.
- I am always asking better and better questions.
- My life is a reflection of my own mind.
- If I am not growing, I am dying.
- I use everything that happens to me in life as an instrument for growth.
- I am a student for life and a student of life.

The 7th Need

The Need for Spirituality

"There is no need for temples; no need for complicated philosophy.
Our own brain, our own heart is our temple."
- Dalai Lama

The universe is a mystical place. Imagine looking into a night sky, looking at the stars knowing that the light you are seeing is so old that it's source may already be gone, looking into infinity and knowing that space goes on and on without an apparent end. Can you ever really say: "I understand"? Or imagine standing on a beach and knowing that no two grains of sand are the same. There is an infinite variety in snow, grass, stones, humanity and life in general. With our mind we try to understand the universe but we find that this is impossible. So we limit ourselves to what the mind can perceive and believe. The reality is that we can never know the underlying principals of the universe unless we go beyond the mind, beyond words and beyond concepts. And even then we are not sure to know the essence. So the question remains, what can we do if we want to know and experience more? If we want to know the ocean we can start examining a drop of water from the ocean. By such an examination we can discover the wetness and the saltiness of the drop. Even if we don't acquire sufficient knowledge of the entire ocean, we have at least acquired an understanding of the underlying principal, because we know the essence of the drop is wetness and saltiness, and that essence in turn makes up the entire ocean. Within the microcosm we find the essence of the macrocosm. This is where the mind must step aside and spiritual practice comes in to play. The inclusion and similar differentiation between the body, mind and soul are universal. According to most spiritual practices the body and mind are vehicles for knowing the soul. Self-knowledge is the highest form of knowledge. Spirituality is an experience beyond the mind.

Religion and spiritual practice

"The state we call realization is simply being oneself,
not knowing anything or becoming anything."
- Ramana Maharshi

In my understanding there is a stark contrast between spiritual practice and religion in many cases. Religion has its dogma. It is mind-based, concept-based and a construction of man. Religion plays a big role in society and fulfills many of the needs already discussed in this book. Religion has given the masses security (a promise of everlasting life and absolution from sins), excitement (singing/chanting/some even include sexual activities), individual strength (my religion is better than yours) and love (everyone is loved within the religion). Religion fulfills all the basic needs and can therefore be almost addictive – or at least extremely popular. I am not downplaying the role of religion in any society. Religion can and does play a very important role for individuals and the society as a whole, but unless there is an emphasis on a *spiritual practice* within the religion (preferably meditation or another form of contemplative practice), it simply *does not* meet the need for spirituality.

Benefits of meditation

"A meditative man has insight.
He can see how he himself created his problems.
And then, naturally he stops creating them."
- Osho

Meditation is a way to gain Self-knowledge through direct perception. In his book *One Taste*, Ken Wilber reports that:

> *"... a regular meditation practice has been clinically proven to evoke the relaxation response, train and strengthen awareness, center and focus the self, halt constant verbal thinking, calm the central nervous system, relieve stress, bolster self-esteem, reduce anxiety and alleviate depression, to name a few; but first and foremost, meditation is a spiritual practice."*

The purpose of meditation is to go beyond the body, beyond the mind, beyond the states of waking and dreaming, and wakefully go into the state of deep sleep or slumber. This has been called *turiya* or the fourth state of consciousness. The mystics have told us that everyone experiences a direct perception of the soul when they are in the state of deep sleep, but when people wake up they are painfully unaware that they have experienced this connection. Most people therefore identify with the limited human body and limited human mind instead of identifying with the eternal soul. This is the cause of most of our suffering. We play small when we have the potential of being one with the ocean of eternity. If human beings identified more with their divine essence and less with their mortal shell it would mean a lessening of fear and a stronger connection to a higher form of consciousness. God is the ocean and our souls are drops of water in that ocean. We are parts of God and God is a part of us. The mystics call out to us and encourage us to meditate so that we can awaken to this fact. They urge us to wake up from the cosmic dream and play our real role in life.

Anyone can have a glimpse of the soul and most people do sometime in their life. Often this happens in a heightened temporary state where body and mind are transcended. But most people don't know how to find their way consciously back to the state of being one with the soul. Meditation is a way to consistently awaken to that connection, to be one with the Self, one with the Ocean and one with God.

There are many paths of meditation to choose from and no use in arguing about which technique is better and which is worse. Meditation is both a practice and a state of consciousness. When you wake up in the morning and go to work, you don't argue with your co-workers about the methods they used to fall asleep the night before in contrast with the method you used. If one falls asleep the method works. Sleep is a state just like meditation. It is something you fall into when the circumstances are right. Arguing about meditation techniques is equally useless as arguing about different methods of falling asleep. If one reaches the state of meditation the technique works. The state of meditation is similar no matter what method is used.

Meditation is such a vast subject. I will offer many resources on the seventh human need at the end of this book but beware of dogma and judgment. Because religion and meditation are so closely related, you may find meditation techniques steeped in dogmatic and fundamentalist philosophy. Be sure to understand that meditation is an experience. It is beyond the body and mind.

The Christian Approach

"There are two main pitfalls on the road to mastery of the art of prayer. If a person gets what he asks for, his humility is in danger. If he fails to get what he asks for, he is apt to lose confidence. Indeed, no matter wheather prayer seems to be succeeding or failing, humility and confidence are two virtues which are absolutely essential."
- A Trappist Monk

Although I have emphasized meditation as a practice so far in this chapter I must also point out that there is another commonly used form of spiritual contemplative practice, namely prayer. Contemplative prayer is very similar to the meditation practice of mantra chanting, mantra repetition or japa. A knowledgeable contemporary teacher is Father Thomas Keating, but in order to emphasize this connection I would like to quote two older books, *The Way of the Pilgrim* and *The Pilgrim Continues His Way*, which record the spiritual pilgrimage of a Russian monk during the middle of the 19th century. This quote has been previously published within the commentary on the Yoga Sutras of Patanjali, in the book *How to Know God* by Swami Prabhavananda and Christopher Isherwood.

The continuous interior Prayer of Jesus is a constant uninterrupted calling upon the divine Name of Jesus with the lips, in the spirit, in the heart; while forming a mental picture of his constant presence, and imploring his grace, during every occupation, at all times, in all places, even during sleep. The appeal is couched in these terms, "Lord Jesus Christ, have mercy on me." One who accustoms himself to this appeal experiences as a result so deep a consolation and so great a need to offer the prayer always, that he can no longer live without it, and it will continue to voice itself within him of its own accord.

Many so-called enlightened people regard this frequent offering of one and the same prayer as useless and even trifling, calling it mechanical and a thoughtless occupation of simple people. But unfortunately they do not know the secret which is revealed as a result of this mechanical exercise, they do not know how this frequent service of the lips imperceptibly becomes a genuine appeal of the heart, sinks down into the inward life, becomes a delight, becomes as it were, natural to the soul, bringing it light and nourishment and leading it on to union with God.

St. John Chrysostom, in his teaching about prayer, speaks as follows: "No one should give the answer that it is impossible for a man occupied with worldly cares, and who is unable to go to church, to pray always. Everywhere, wherever you may find yourself, you can set up an altar to God in your mind by means of prayer. And so it is fitting to pray at your trade, on a journey, standing at the counter or sitting at your handicraft .... In such an order of life all his actions, by the power of the invocation of the Name of God, would be signalized by success, and finally he would train himself to uninterrupted prayerful invocation of the Name of Jesus Christ. He would come to know from experience that frequency of prayer, this sole means to salvation, is a possibility for the will of man, that it is possible to pray at all times, in all circumstances and in every place, and easily to rise from frequent vocal prayer to prayer of the mind and from that to prayer of the heart, which opens up the Kingdom of God within us."

Self-knowledge

"Put your heart, mind, intellect, and soul
even to your smallest acts. This is the secret of success."
- Swami Sivananda

Pursuing Self-knowledge is the primary goal of life. All other goals are secondary and should support the primary goal. Balancing the six previous human needs is a very important secondary goal but one should not get lost in the pursuit of any of those needs at the cost of not experiencing the Self, the Soul, the Divine, the Atman.

Many mystics, yogis, monks and spiritual masters over the ages have proclaimed to be able to meet all the seven human needs through intense spiritual practice. According to the scriptures the masters have found absolute security within the realm of the eternal Soul (1st need). To them, nothing is more exciting than a connection to this higher power; it is absolute truth, knowledge and love (2nd need). When a drop of water experiences oneness with the ocean, the drop feels like it has all the power of the ocean behind him and therefore the masters have found an inexhaustible reservoir of individual strength through spiritual practice (3rd need). The love of the Soul/Self/ God is absolute; to the masters it is the ultimate love relationship (4th need). Once they have made this connection, an expression of ultimate truth flows from their lips, and through their lives; they proclaim to see the soul/God in everyone and want to be of service to humanity (5th need). In this state of bliss the masters have acquired the ultimate knowledge, Self-knowledge, knowledge that death cannot take away (6th need). All this and more the mystics claim to have acquired through the spiritual practice of meditation (7th need).

Spirituality is not a myth, far away or unreachable. It is your birthright. It is within your reach, within your grasp. Know it, feel it and practice it.

Knowledge in and of itself is not enough, contemplation is not enough, being inspired in the presence of a master is not enough - to realize your true Self you must practice meditation or any other form of contemplation. But meditation must be accompanied with a balance of all the other needs, especially compassion and care. Otherwise spiritual practice can become mechanical. Remember - spiritual connection is the primary goal of life, it gives you the possibility to live from a higher perspective, the perspective of the everlasting Soul.

Out of Balance

Any form of imbalance connected to the previous six needs will show up in spiritual practice. Re-read the imbalances connected to the previous needs and you will get a clearer picture of everything that can possibly go wrong. This is why, according to Ken Wilber, any dedicated practitioner should take up some form of an integral practice, including at least exercise, cognitive training, emotional growth and meditation. This form of cross training will minimize imbalance and maximize results. "The Darth Vader move is always possible," as Wilber puts it (in a reference to the movie *Star Wars*). The more evolved and complex a human being is the more things can go wrong. Any of the imbalances discussed in this book are ever present and always possible. The meditation practitioner must be forever vigilant and keep on balancing the seven human needs. Nobody is perfect – we are our actions at any moment, nothing more. However spiritually evolved a human being has become; anyone can turn around at any point and start acting in a destructive and sinful way the next day. It's kind of like cultivating a garden. You can tend to a garden everyday for 20, 30 or 40 years. But if one day you stop giving it loving attention and care through your actions it will rapidly deteriorate. Weeds will start to grow and in a relatively short period of time the garden will become a jungle. On the other hand, it is much easier to turn around and start cultivating the garden once again, if it has flourished in the past. The same is true with the human mind and respectively the actions we take every day. If we cultivate our life with dedication, positive thinking and consistent actions, it will be much easier to turn away from destructive behavior, however far we stray away from our original course.

The ultimate deficiency in relation to the spiritual need is denial. A person that denies the spiritual connection is in reality denying an ever present and all pervading part of him- or herself. The consciousness present in the state of deep sleep is not of a cognitive or mental kind or else we would have memory of it when we wake up. But this consciousness is always present; it's also there in the states of dreaming and waking. Within that context, consciousness has been called the *ever present witness*. Denying the witness and not taking the time to experience the deep sleep consciousness wakefully is the mark of imbalance in relation to spirituality. This is the case for many people, in fact it's the case for most of the people that don't meditate (and even some that do). Cognitive understanding does not equal experience. Ramana Maharishi told his disciples that whatever is not present in the state of deep sleep is not real. What he meant was that this witness consciousness is the only part of a human being that is always present and eternal. This timeless truth has been expounded upon by all spiritual masters. Within every human being there is an ever present and eternal witness waiting to be uncovered. But while the waves of the mind are turbulent one cannot see to the depths of the ocean. The waves must subside in order for one to see the depth.

Through a steady meditation practice one can build a strong bond between the mind and soul, but without meditation, contemplative prayer or some other form of yoga (yoking together the body/mind/soul) there is little or no hope for this experience. Much of the turmoil and emptiness that springs up from within a person's being is a longing for a reunion with the soul. If a person searches outwardly for fulfillment it will forever elude him. But by harmonizing oneself with the outside world (balancing the first six needs) one can turn more attention inward and within a moment one can experience this ever present Self and be happy, free and blissful.

Practical advice

1. Learn how to meditate or start some kind of a contemplative practice

Learning meditation is easy – but practicing every day takes cultivation, dedication and discipline. If you decide to do it, make it a consistent habit – one that is easy to live with. The simplest form of meditation is the observation of breath or the repetition of a prayer or mantra. Sit still for 10-20 minutes at a time (you can even set a timer) and observe the breath or repeat a prayer or mantra. Allow the mind to calm down and concentrate. Whenever the mind wonders, focus on the breath once more. Do this repeatedly and stay with it. Yogi Hari explains further in his book *Sampoorna Yoga*:

"When concentration is maintained unbroken for about two minutes, one naturally falls into meditation. At this stage, there is no more awareness of space and time. In theory, any object could

be chosen as a point of focus, but the choice has to be made very carefully because whatever you focus on is going to impregnate your subconscious and a concentrated mind has the power to bring thoughts to the point of manifestation. That is why spiritual aspirants are advised to concentrate on God, so that divine qualities may manifest themselves. Meditation is then defined as "the constant flow of thoughts toward God." It cannot be achieved. You fall into it when the conditions are ready, meaning, when the mind is one-pointed and steady."

2. Find a spiritual master, teacher or guide

If you want to learn anything of importance you will need a master or a teacher, at least a guide. Books will not suffice if you want to become proficient. The same is true with spiritual practice and spiritual philosophy. I further emphasize this point by quoting the spiritual master Omraam Mikhael Aivanhov from his book titled, *What is a spiritual master?*

"You never hear of any great musician who has reached the top of his profession without having had a teacher. The same thing applies in the spiritual world. If you do not have a Master, it is very difficult for you to keep persevering. You think that it would be good for you to meditate and make efforts to improve, but very quickly your old habits creep in. A few months later, you remember all your good intentions, and once again you start trying... until the day when you finally fall back into inertia. However, if you have a Master, you feel continuously stimulated; he draws you along both by his words and his example. He touches your feelings and because you love and admire him, you are pushed to work on transforming yourself."

Here in the West much controversy has arisen around the ideas of spiritual masters and rightly so. Many men and women have posed as spiritual masters and done great harm within the society as a result. Finding a spiritual master is not easy at all. You could start by searching for a teacher, at least someone that is further along the spiritual path than you are. Just remember that everyone has to go to the toilet. What does that mean? It means that everyone is human. In his book *One Taste* Ken Wilber explains:

"You can be at a relatively high level of spiritual development and still be at a relatively low level in other lines (e.g., the deeper psychic can be progressing while the frontal is quite retarded). We all know people who are spiritually developed but still rather immature in sexual relations, emotional intimacy, physical health and so on."

It is my belief that myths of spiritual masters as perfect human beings have done more harm than good in society. While looking for what you may perceive as a spiritual master (and in many cases the search is a mere reflection of your own likes and dislikes) you may overlook a simple and profound teacher that could easily guide you along the spiritual path. When the student is ready the teacher will appear. The role of a spiritual master is to help his students stand on their own two feet. His role is not to make them dependent on him. A true spiritual master is a shape shifter. He uses different methods for different people, according to where they are situated on the spiritual path.

Questions to help you grow

· Who am I?
· What is the spiritual purpose of my life?
· Do I really want to know my Self?
· Where can I learn how to meditate?
· How can I balance my external life
  to further evolve in my meditation practice?
· How can I put insights gained through
  a steady meditation practice to good use?

Affirmations

Serve, Love, Give, Purify, Meditate, Realize.
- Swami Sivananda

I have taken the affirmations and negations relating to this chapter from the book *Dynamic Balanced Living* by Yogi Shanti Desai with his consent. First come negations (I am not this, I am not that). They are followed by affirmations relating to the ever present Self. I recommend that you read these along with your meditation practice every day.

Negations

· *I have no race or nationality.*
  The human race is my nationality.
· *I have no religion. Dharma is my universal religion.*
· *I have no dogma or beliefs.*
  The divine light removes my ignorance.
· *I have no family. All living creatures are my family members.*
· *I have no home. The entire universe is my home.*
· *I have no fame or power.*
  All I have is a small reflection of the divine.

· *I own nothing.*
Everything is provided, as necessary, by the divine.
· *I possess no one.*
I am here to serve others for my purification and evolution.
· *I control nothing. I am only an instrument.*
Cosmic laws govern everything.
· *I rely on nothing and no one.*
I rely on divine grace and satsang.
· *I am not the intellect. I rely on divine grace and intuition.*
· *I am not the emotions. They change constantly.*
· *I am free from duality. Free from pleasure-pain,*
gain-loss, honor-insult.
· *I am not the mind. Mind does not exist.*
Mind is the changing waves.
· *I am not the senses.*
They are only means of perception and action.
· *I am not the body.*
It is vibrating energy which changes constantly.
· *I am not male or female. I am the spirit without boundaries.*
· *I am not a father, brother, son, mother or sister.*
These are the roles I play.
· *I have no name. Name is just a label.*

Affirmations

· *I am the Self (Atman): Spark of God as Sat, Chit and Anand.*
· *I am the bliss consciousness:*
  Uninvolved passive witness to the drama of life.
· *I am immortal: Never born, never dying.*
  I am sustained by the divine energy.
· *I have nothing to attain, nothing to be, nowhere to go.*
· *I am perfect, self-sufficient and content:*
  I need nothing added to life.
· *I am perfect and free, here and now:*
  Nothing or nobody binds me.

Living in Line with the Seven Human Needs

"The fear of death follows from the fear of life.
A man who lives fully is prepared to die at any time."
- Mark Twain

How to apply
the Seven Human Needs

"Always dream and shoot higher than you know how to.
Don't bother just to be better than your contemporaries or predecessors.
Try to be better than yourself."
– William Faulkner

There are infinite ways to apply the seven human needs to all areas of life. The most obvious, and the one that this book has revolved around for the most part, is self improvement. It should be clear to the reader that a continuous act of balancing the seven human needs is the foundation for a peaceful mind, happiness and harmony. However, it must also be recognized that the ratio between the needs will constantly change during life's journey.

I like the stage model taught in yoga philosophy. The first stage of life consists of learning and strengthening one's own character. One is taught the basics connected to all the seven human needs, both material and spiritual truths. The first stage is about building a strong foundation that can then be integrated into the later stages of life. The second stage of life consists of raising a family and being prosperous so that one doesn't become a burden on society. In the third stage of life a person should be able to serve society and even humanity at large. The children are grown up and enough material wealth should have been gathered to provide for a healthy retirement. The fourth and final stage of life should, according to this model, be spent in seclusion or at least in some diminished form of worldly activity, while contemplating the divine through meditation and introspection. If you apply this model to your life you will be content at which ever stage you are, instead of wishing that you could spend less time in material pursuits and more time pursuing spiritual practice or vice versa.

People with intense spiritual inclinations always have the possibility of retiring from the material world sooner; taking monastic vows in an ashram, abbey or temple, but for the average spiritually-inclined human being, the model of the four stages of life makes sense.

Relationships

"'Tis better to have loved and lost
than never to have loved at all."
- Alfred, Lord Tennyson

Applying the seven human needs to relationships means that two people must first balance the needs within themselves and then balance the needs with each other. Here are some points on what can be done to fulfill the seven human needs within a relationship.

To fulfill the need for security, both persons must be fully committed to the relationship and work on its unity. A lack of commitment is a common complaint when it comes to relationships, so the first step for any relationship is for the parties concerned to know what they want and then commit to resolving any differences that will inevitably arise.

Secondly, both persons need to know how to keep each other excited, by being creatively and sexually active. The only real difference between a loving friendship and a romantic relationship is the sexual connection. If that is lost, frustration and disappointment can lead to repression, and after having read about the second need you know what kind of trouble that can cause. Balancing the need for excitement between two people in an intimate relationship is a never ending dance where both people have to stay alert and have fun. The most common complaint couples have today is: "Where did the excitement go?" This need can be met through various practices and the passion between two people can be kept alive. Even though the second need can be hard to control and may even turn animalistic in its imbalanced form it should never be discarded or subdued if a relationship is meant to last.

Regarding the third and fourth needs both individuals in the relationship need to maintain their own identity while being constantly open to giving and receiving love. As discussed earlier in this book the balancing act is not easy and visible contradictions sometimes seem insurmountable. But these are the cards we have been dealt in life and we must pursue the balancing act if we want to have a successful relationship.

Every relationship should also have an open channel of communication and expression and a way for the couple to contribute beyond their own meager surroundings.

In a relationship one should constantly be open to more ways to grow, expand love and increase the understanding within the relationship. It's hard work, but it is worth every drop of sweat perspired in its pursuit.

Finding a rhythm within the relationship where both people can pursue their spiritual inclinations is very important. If both people share the same inclination for meditation and spiritual growth it's a real blessing for the relationship. A parallel spiritual practice can form a satsang or support system within the home. If not, there should be understanding and respect between the two people in this area of life.

Raising a child

"The greatest good you can do for another
is not just to share your riches, but to reveal to him his own."
- Benjamin Disraeli

It stands to reason that you should bring the same awareness to raising a child as you would to your own self development. Providing the child with secure surroundings, not repressing its natural inclination for excitement and creativity, helping the child build and maintain self-confidence and self-esteem, giving him unconditional love, teaching the child to express himself and contribute, constantly helping him increase his cognitive capacity and providing the child with methods of pursuing a spiritual connection, such as prayer and meditation, are just some of the ways in which you can apply the seven human needs to upbringing. Be creative and playful while helping the child grow and evolve. Our children can be raised to our own level of consciousness and they should be able to evolve beyond that in their lifetime. Our children should be able to stand on our shoulders.

Money and Work

"Happiness seems to require a modicum of external prosperity."
- *Aristotle*

The human needs hierarchy and psychology of Abraham Maslow is taught in all marketing, sales and business education. The seven human needs can be exploited for profit (we all know that tapping into imbalanced needs for security, excitement and individual strength is big business, both legal and illegal) or they can be used to serve people – and in the later case everyone profits. If you want to create a win-win situation, where everyone prospers, why not find positive and constructive ways to meet more needs and profit from that kind of service? If you are in business or want to go into business, ask yourself: "What can be done constructively to fulfill the needs for security, excitement, creativity, individual strength, love, relationships, expression, contribution, wisdom, growth and spiritual connection?" The more needs you can meet with your products or services, the more profits you can make without compromising your integrity.

Politics

"The mass of men lead lives of quiet desperation."
- *Henry David Thoreau*

If you look at the balance between the seven human needs, it seems that all inclinations in politics are right or at least not a hundred percent wrong. Finding a balance between left and right wings in politics and letting both sides have their say about the way a society should be run could turn out to be very beneficial. By applying the seven human needs to politics the politicians could provide security and stability for their voters, ways for pursuing excitement without many of the detrimental effects, freedom of action within a disciplined framework in order to pursue individual strength and entrepreneurship, compassion and support for those not able to fend for themselves, a strong social framework for families, freedom of expression, an educational system providing knowledge and growth and the freedom to pursue any spiritual path. Some countries already meet many of the needs within their current constitutional framework. The above mentioned ideas can be a starting point. I don't pretend to have all the answers, but if you want to go into politics ask yourself this question: "How can I be of service and produce a framework that will give a majority of my countrymen the social surroundings and the freedom to pursue all of the seven human needs equally?"

This short overview of how to apply the seven human needs is in no means conclusive or exhaustive. Use introspection, imagination, observation and contemplation to find more ways to apply the seven human needs to your life and the lives of the people around you.

Find your Center Of Gravity and Cultivate Your Strength

"Man, alone, has the power to transform his thoughts into physical reality; man, alone, can dream and make his dreams come true."
– Napoleon Hill

In my lectures on the seven human needs, many people have become daunted and even discouraged when facing a task they perceive as enormous: the task of balancing the seven human needs. This is natural and normal, but totally unnecessary. You do not have to perform at the highest level within each need to be fulfilled. Just take one step at a time. Cultivating awareness and giving the needs some attention will bring about much of the required change. But we all have a center of gravity of sorts, a central need we gravitate towards in our life. If you have found your strength within this framework I applaud you and encourage you to keep on building on that strength. But that also means giving some attention to the other needs in order to lead a balanced life. If you have not found your unique strength yet, you should examine your life and contemplate the needs in order to find you center of gravity. This may in fact be your life's purpose.

One way to find your center of gravity is to be aware of how you feel and react when you read about the needs explained in this book. Whatever need you have felt the most strongly and passionately about may be your center of gravity. The opposite may also be true. Wherever you lost interest or felt resistance to the material being presented may be you weakness within the context of the seven human needs. This method, however, is not a full proof way of determining your strengths and weaknesses, although it may give you an indication.

All my life I have gravitated towards the need for expression and contribution. At first it was based on selfish desires. In my late teens and early twenties I wanted to become a famous rock star, singer or actor. Then I turned my life around and became a yoga teacher, a speaker and a writer. I gravitate towards more ways of helping more people enhance their own quality of life while I am growing all the time myself. I place much emphasis on the other six needs but I always find myself expressing or contributing much of what I have learned in one way or another. That is the primary reason why you are holding this book in your hands at this very moment. Whatever I have learned about the seven needs seems to find its way to the public through some form of expression, be it a lecture, audio program, book or a newspaper article, to name a few.

Child of God

Here is a passage by Marianne Williamson that has incorrectly been attributed to Nelson Mandela through the years. It is a passage of great inspiration and should encourage you to find your own center of gravity and strength in life.

"Our deepest fear is not that we are inadequate.
Our deepest fear is that we are powerful beyond measure.
It is our light, not our darkness, that most frightens us.
We ask ourselves, who am I to be brilliant,
gorgeous, talented, and fabulous?
Actually, who are you not to be?
You are a child of God.
Your playing small doesn't serve the world.
There's nothing enlightened about shrinking so
that other people won't feel insecure around you.
We are all meant to shine, as children do.
We are born to make manifest the glory of God
that is within us.
It's not just in some of us, it's in everyone.
And as we let our own light shine,
we unconsciously give other
people permission to do the same.
As we are liberated from our own fear,
our presence automatically liberates others."

Past and Future Approaches to Spirituality

"The ultimate measure of a man
is not where he stands in moments of comfort,
but where he stands in times of challenge and controversy."
– Martin Luther King, Jr.

So what is the highest ideal? Should we emulate the spiritual masters of the past or should we try to find a new holistic or integral way of balancing the needs and live from the perspective of the soul? What does it feel like to be enlightened? What does it look like? These are all valid questions. The traditions tell us to emulate the masters, to find a guru or teacher and take on all of his traits. But what if a master is highly evolved on a spiritual level and a complete jerk in his human interactions? Is this scenario possible? Of course it is. As already stated in this book there are various examples. But what should we do then?

In yoga there is a practice called *viveka* or spiritual discrimination that has come to be very important in our times. In the modern world we have access to all the spiritual practices of all the so-called wisdom traditions of the world to date. This can be highly disorienting and can even lead to a breakdown when a person is exposed to so many seemingly contradicting truths and doesn't know which one to follow. That is why the integral approach is so important. An integral approach centers on trying to find the universal truths and similarities, instead of being hung up on the differences. The most exhaustive research and writing in this area has been done by Ken Wilber. I recommend all of his books and most of them are mentioned in the resource section at the end of this book.

Let us now turn back to the question of emulating a master. If we have knowledge of the seven human needs we should be able to distinguish between the balanced and imbalanced areas of the master. However, having said that I must remind you that a true master is a shape shifter, who sometimes takes on the role of a jerk for educational or teaching purposes without being stuck there himself. Having spiritual discrimination is not black and white, but closer to shades of grey. If we can distinguish, we can emulate the most beneficial, constructive and positive traits of a master. But then there arise questions to further complicate this issue. If we can discriminate and choose a master, do we really need his guidance? If we can *choose* our master, have we not become masters ourselves? This is tricky business. In the end, it's up to us to decide. If we don't try, we can't know.

Stains on a white piece of cloth

"The person who seeks all their applause from the outside has their happiness in another's keeping."
- Dale Carnegie

We must also remember that stains on a white piece of cloth are very visible. It is often the case that the people we call spiritual masters or masters of life have done much washing of their own cloth (character) but the few stains that are left over have become very visible in contrast to the white background. On the other hand we often praise the people who have just started their personal development because we start seeing some white spots on an otherwise dirty cloth. The practice of compassion and tolerance is very important when learning from another human being. The student's mindset determines the outcome of any learning situation.

The highest ideal has been called by many names, including enlightenment, *nirvana*, samadhi, *turiya*, bliss and Self-realization, to name a few. But these are all symbols of internal states of consciousness that can't be measured by the outside world, even though some of these states seem to have corresponding brain wave functions that can be measured.

When a person decides to follow the advice of a teacher or emulate a guru or spiritual master it can only be done through *faith*. The person must have faith in the teachings in order to follow the disciplines and put in the practice needed to gain the benefits. Trust and faith are internal features. If you find trust and faith within – follow the path with all your heart, put in the practice and see where it leads you.

Personal Practice

"If you don't use ordinary life as a method to meditation,
your meditation is bound to become something of an escape.
If your ordinary life becomes extraordinary,
only then are you spiritual."
- Zen

If you want to form a regular practice around the seven human needs and incorporate some of the disciplines into your daily or weekly schedule you can include many of the practices already discussed in this book. However I would like to remind you of the basics.

It should come as no surprise that I recommend seven disciplines to form an integral or holistic personal practice.

1. Exercise. All the research being done in this area suggests that regular exercise has numerous benefits at the physical, mental and emotional levels. The experts advise the following: Weight lifting, hatha yoga (stretching) and/or aerobic exercise (preferably with a heart rate monitor). A combination of all three has proven to be most beneficial.

2. Financial management. Manage your money and spend some time, every day or every week, going over the numbers. Save and invest. Whatever gets measured gets managed.

3. Creativity. Find consistent outlets for your creative energy.

4. Self-development. Use affirmations, control your inner dialogue through questions, strengthen your self-identity and self-image and associate with positive and constructive people.

5. Emotional management and moral development. Learn to manage your emotions and increase your moral understanding through therapy, discussion groups, reading or other forms of communication and introspection.

6. Increase you intellectual and cognitive capacity. Read or listen to something that expands your mind (preferably something that leaves stretch marks) every day. Challenge yourself and your mental capabilities.

7. Meditate every day. Research has shown that regular meditation is the fastest way to grow and evolve in all areas of life.

My recommendations in this chapter on personal practice have been inspired by Ken Wilber's integral model. Within that model he emphasizes four areas called ITP (Integral Transformative Practice). They are exercise, emotional understanding, cognitive capacity and meditation. Here is a short description from his book *One Taste*:

"So even as you advance in you own spiritual unfolding, consider combining it with a good psychotherapeutic practice, because spiritual practice, as a rule, will not adequately expose the psychodynamic unconscious. Nor will it appropriately exercise the physical body – so try weightlifting. Nor will it exercise the pranic body – try adding t'ai chi ch'uan. Nor will it work with group or community dynamic, so add... Well, the point of course, is to take up integral practice as the only sound and balanced way to proceed with one's own higher development."

Since much of my material is based on yoga philosophy (see epilogue), I would like to include a very short description of how an integral, holistic or *Sampoorna* (full) approach to yoga can help you balance the seven human needs.

Raja yoga – This is a classical eight limbed practice, including moral development, physical posture, breath control, sense withadrawal, concentration, meditation and blissful union. The practice is aimed at restraining the animalistic tendencies of the survival instinct (1st need), sensuality (2nd need) and egoic selfishness (3rd need) through morality, trancendance and practice. Concentration and meditation are used to move beyond the mind (7th need). Raja yoga has been called the scientific method.

Bhakti yoga – Is the devotional aspect of yoga. You use love and devotion (4th need) to rise above destructive emotions and eventually rise above the mind (7th need).

Gnana yoga – In this approach you use the intellect (6th need) to derive wisdom about the true nature of the Self (7th need).

Karma yoga – Action is used (1st, 3rd and 5th needs) to live and interact with the world without attachments to the outcome (7th need).

Hatha yoga – Is the science of health (1st need) and energy (2nd and 3rd needs) and includes physical postures, breathing and relaxation.

Nada yoga – Is based on mantra chanting and devotional singing. It is the science of vibration (5th need) and should be used to elevate the mind (7th need).

By integrating all these aspects of yoga you have a Sampoorna (full) practice that can help you balance the seven human needs and even lead you to a permanent state of health, happiness and a peaceful mind. In the words of Yogi Hari: "Each individual is as full as the fullness, the pure consciousness from which he comes.".

Growth - Living From a New Perspective

"Consider the world as a school to learn spiritual lessons.
All souls are in different grades and at different levels of evolution.
Accept them and love them.
Do not impose your ideas and models on others."
- Yogi Shanti Desai

The seven human needs practical philosophy seems to develop in a hierarchy or holarchy, which ever concept you prefer. A hierarchy is one thing built on top of another, a holarchy is a whole with parts included in another whole, just like cells build on molecules and molecules build on atoms, but they are all a part of a larger whole. Applying this to the seven human needs means that the need for spiritual connection builds on the need for security and so on and so forth. I refer back to the book *Mans Search for Meaning* by Viktor Frankl for corroboration. Many of the prisoners in Nazi concentration camps were stripped of all needs but the need for security and survival through extreme circumstances. Frankl states that there were no acts of sodomy in these camps. Nowhere but in the most extreme conditions can the sexual drive be stripped away. The last remaining need was the survival instinct and therefore it can be called the foundation of the hierarchy. The way to build a healthy hierarchy/holarchy is to build the foundation first and then transcend and include each of the succeeding and previous components or needs. This is what constitutes as growth in the model for the seven human needs. Growth is being able to use and balance all the previous needs, yet at the same time live from a higher perspective or a higher center of gravity. This statement may seem to contradict the previous chapter on finding your center of gravity and cultivating your strength, but in essence it does not. You can live from the highest perspective of the soul and still work at a bank, since financial knowledge is your strength.

Another way to look at the hierarchy/holarchy is that you can grow through the moral stages of selfish, to care, to universal care, all the way to integral, within each of the seven human needs. You can start out as selfishly secure, caringly creative, selfishly strong and so on. At the final stage of growth you can become integrally secure, creative, strong, loving, expressive, wise and spiritual. In that respect each need can become a line of development in it self. M. Scott Peck gives a similar growth model for the spiritual seeker in his book *Further along the Road Less Traveled*. I quote:

"Stage One, which I label chaotic/antisocial and which may be thought of as a stage of lawlessness, absent of spirituality; Stage Two, which I label formal/institutional and which may be thought of as rigorous adherence to the letter of the law and attachment to the forms of religion; Stage Three, which I label skeptic/individual and which is a stage of principled behavior, but one characterized by religious doubt or disinterest, albeit accompanied by inquisitiveness about other areas of life; And finally Stage Four, the most mature

of the stages, which I label mystical/communal and which may be thought of as a state of the spirit of the law, as opposed to Stage Two, which tends to be one of the letter of the law.

You may quickly see parallels between these stages of spiritual development and the psychosexual developmental stages with which psychiatrists are generally familiar – Stage One corresponding in some ways to the first five years of life, Stage two the latency period, Stage Three to adolescence and early adulthood, and Stage Four to the last half of life in healthy human development. And like developmental stages, the stages of spiritual development are sequential. They cannot be skipped over, there are people in between stages, and there are gradations within stages."

If you overlap the models of psychosexual development (standard psychiatry), moral development (selfish/care/world care/integral) and spiritual development (Peck) they appear very similar in meaning, even though different words and symbols are used.

This can be taken to mean that any form of healthy personal growth must evolve from a narcissistic and chaotic level, to a formal, disciplined and caring level, based on security and rules. From there a person can start raising his or her awareness. This then leads to skeptic questioning, scientific inquiry and contemplation. Through that practice a person can evolve to a level of universal care and finally the spiraling development comes to its pinnacle with the mystical, communal and integral level.

This hierarchical development can happen either within a particular need or in relation to the seven human needs as a hierarchy of their own.

One additional way to look at the seven human needs is as the seven most important intelligences (in line with the multiple intelligence model of Dr. Howard Gardner). If I would apply his verbiage to my material, this book could have been called the seven human intelligences. As a result the needs would have been given different names, such as:

1. Survival intelligence.
2. Sensual intelligence.
3. Character intelligence.
4. Emotional intelligence.
5. Expressional intelligence.
6. Intellectual intelligence.
7. Spiritual intelligence.

I bring this up as a way to expand your mind and to point out that the seven human needs is just a label I have made up to provide you with a practical mapping mechanism. The information remains the same, even if the labels were to change. It is as Shakespeare wrote in his play about Romeo and Juliet, when Juliet says: "What's in a name? That which we call a rose by any other name would smell as sweet."

What is Your Next Step?

"I do not think much of a man who is not wiser today
than he was yesterday."
– Abraham Lincoln

Let me remind you of the challenge in the beginning of this book: Read about *one need every day (seven needs/seven days)*, especially the practical advice, questions and affirmations, for the next few weeks or months and see where it leads you.

It is my firm belief that if you bring the seven human needs into your daily awareness and make them a part of your life you will reap great rewards. Balancing the needs, finding your center of gravity and cultivating your strength can yield a consistent increase to your growth and understanding. Through repetition, even if you only stay aware of the highlights, the framework of the seven human needs will impregnate your subconscious mind; it will become a *part of who you are* and your life will seek balance and harmony, almost of its own accord.

My own understanding of the seven human needs is increasing daily, both through contemplation, research and human interaction. I have certainly not reached a state of permanent balance. I am a work in progress and I regularly become pessimistic, irritable and forget to follow most of the disciplines outlined in this book. But my knowledge and awareness of the seven human needs has given me great tools that make it easier for me to find balance when I move into the extremities of life. It takes me less time to rebound than it did before. This can be true for you as well.

I have done my best to present this material in an easy to use and practical manner. What you do now is up to you and you alone. If you have been inspired, take action. Start you journey towards greater balance, health, happiness and peace of mind. If you need more assistance please visit my website, www.sevenhumanneeds.com, for resources, insights, audio commentaries and success stories.

Gudjon Bergmann,
gudjon@gbergmann.is
www.sevenhumanneeds.com
Iceland, May, 2006

P.S. Please send me a letter or e-mail containing a few words about how your personal practice is going once you get into it. Your story might find its way onto my website or even become a part of a future publication and serve as inspiration for others who are just now beginning the journey of finding balance and harmony between the seven human needs.

Epilogue

"What we call the beginning is often the end.
And to make an end is to make a beginning.
The end is where we start from."
- T.S. Eliot

Where do the Seven Human needs come from?

"I am like a little pencil in God's hand.
He does the writing. The pencil has nothing to do with it."
- Mother Teresa

When I started practicing and then teaching yoga almost ten years ago, I became fascinated with the philosophy and found that I was especially interested in the ideology of the chakra system. For those who don't already know, the chakras are the so called energy wheels of the astral/energy body associated with yoga. Yoga philosophy divides the human being into three bodies, material, astral and causal, and according to the masters of yoga, these bodies should be yoked together or united for a person to achieve wholeness (holiness). Although I have never actually seen a chakra or any of the colors associated with the system with my own eyes, the congruency of many spiritual masters I have read about and met through the years has made me less skeptical about their actual existence. To me the chakras are powerful and practical *symbols* that correspond with the human body, mind and soul. In the year 2002 I wrote a little verse called *Find Balance through the Chakras* in Icelandic. There I started to formulate the ideology of the needs. Much of the reading material I have come across since has corroborated my initial intuition about the seven human needs embedded in the symbology of the chakras. I have found that the work of Abraham Maslow can almost be superimposed over the chakra system as I will attempt to do later in this chapter. Last year I attended an Anthony Robbins seminar, *Unleash the Power Within*, in London. His formula of the six human emotional needs was exactly the inspiration I needed to conclude the philosophy of the seven human needs contained in this book. Let me now compare the needs with these ideologies to show you the origins of the seven human needs.

Why seven?

"It is doubtless a vice to turn one's eyes inward too much,
but I am my own comedy and tragedy."
- Ralph Waldo Emerson

There are seven chakras and so there are seven needs. My model is a simplification for practical purposes. Much deeper meaning can be read into the chakra system by advanced masters. However, the needs could probably be split up into more or less categories: Plato devised three categories that control human behaviour (desire, emotion and knowledge); Abraham Maslow devised five (see comparison to the hierarchy); and Anthony Robbins teaches the six human needs in his seminars (certainty, uncertainty, significance, love, contribution and growth).

Let me now compare the needs to the chakra system. According to eastern philosophy the chakras or energy wheels are situated along the spine. The first chakra is placed at the base of the spine, signifying the foundation and need for security (the first need). The second chakra is placed close to the sexual organs, expressing the need for creation and excitement (the second need). The third chakra is placed close to the solar plexus, which is a bundle of nerves just above the navel and below the diaphragm, representing nerve energy and individual strength (the third need). The fourth chakra is placed close to the heart, representing the need for love, emotions and closeness with other people (the fourth need). The fifth chakra is placed at the bottom of the throat, which is our center of expression, and is also symbolic for our need for contribution (the fifth need). The sixth chakra is situated in the center of the forehead, symbolizing the need for wisdom and growth (the sixth need). Most eastern meditation practices direct the practitioner to focus his or her attention on the front of the forehead when learning to concentrate and meditate. In evolutionary terms it seems that the frontal lobes of the brain are a big part of the physical distinctions that make us uniquely human. In fact they are the most recently added attribute to the human brain. Research done on Buddhist monks, that have meditated for ten to fifty thousand hours in their lifetime, show that their frontal lobes light up (in an EEG machine) when the monks enter a blissful meditative state of consciousness. They also seem to augment the brain's gamma waves when mastering such emotions as anger (Scientific American March 2006). Another memory expert I listened to recently said that most of our long term memory and emotional instincts can be found in the middle part of our brain, so the very act of focusing on the frontal lobes can bring awareness away from the thoughts and emotions of the past that cause much of our distress. The seventh chakra is then said to be placed just above the top of the head, symbolizing the need for the connection between the body and higher consciousness, a Biblical connection between heaven and earth, symbolizing the need for spirituality (the seventh need).

Maslow's hierarchy

"We are not in a position in which we have nothing to work with.
We already have capacities, talents, direction, missions, callings."
- Abraham Maslow

Then there is the comparison to Abraham Maslows hierarchy of needs, even though his system consists of only five levels. According to Maslow the first level consists of survival or physiological needs, the most primitive of all needs, consisting of the basic animal requirements such as food, water, shelter, warmth and sleep. The second level consist of security or safety needs. In earlier times these needs were expressed as a desire to be free of physical danger. This need has been refined so that its implications are now felt in terms of the social and financial, such as job security, rather than purely physical requirements. These first two levels correspond with the first and second needs of the seven found in this book. His third level consists of social needs, to belong and be accepted by others. This level corresponds with the fourth need for love and relationships, not to be confused with Maslow's fourth level, which consists of ego-status needs, to be held in esteem by both oneself and others. This kind of need is satisfied by power, prestige and self-confidence. The fourth level corresponds with the third need for individual strength in this book. His fifth and last level consist of self-actualization needs, to maximize one's skills and talents. This embraces self-realization, self-expression and self-fulfillment. His fifth level corresponds with the fifth, sixth and seventh needs within the seven already discussed in this book.

Resources

"God prefers bad verses recited with a pure heart
to the finest verses chanted by the wicked."
- Voltaire

For in depth reading and listening, I have put together a list of the most influential and constructive material I have come across in my life so far. Because of the scope and quality of some of the material, I may recommend the same books or audio programs more than once within the frame of the needs. The list is not meant to be conclusive, so please let me know if you would like to recommend any other material that might be useful for in depth reading. You can also visit my website www.sevenhumanneeds.com for more resources, including links to websites, links to the books recommended (if you want to buy them), magazines I recommend and DVD's that could be helpful.

If you join our *mailing list* you will receive a printable *A4 poster* with an overview of the seven human needs. Hang the poster up in plain sight to remind you of all the needs, their pitfalls and their promises. I plan to keep my website active, so in the future you may find more in depth material, including audio commentary, articles, interviews, the seven human needs test and much more.

1. The Need for Security

Health - Books

- *The Future of the Body* – Michael Murphy
- *Yoga Holistic Practice Manual* – Yogi Shanti Desai
- *Sampoorna Yoga* – Yogi Hari
- *Your Body's Many Cries for Water* – F. Batmanghelidj, M.D.
- *The Energy Balance Diet* – Joshua Rosenthal with Tom Monte
- *You: The Owners Manual* – Michael F. Roizen, M.D. and Mehmet C. Oz, M.D.
- *Body Mind Mastery* – Dan Millman
- *Harmony and Health* – Omraam Mikhaël Aïvahov
- *Perfect Health* – Deepak Chopra
- *Ayurveda: The Science of Self Healing* – Dr. Vasant Lad
- *Gesundheit!* – Patch Adams M.D.
- *The Relaxation Response* – Herbert Benson
- *Slow Burn* – Stu Mittleman

Health - Audio Programs

- *Magical Mind, Magical Body* – Deepak Chopra
- *The Body You Deserve* – Anthony Robbins

Finances - Books

- *The Richest Man in Babylon* – George S. Clason
- *Think and Grow Rich* – Napoleon Hill
- *The Seven Spiritual Laws of Success* – Deepak Chopra
- *Rich Dad, Poor Dad* – Robert Kiyosaki
- *Keys to the Vault* – Keith Cunningham

Environmental Issues - Books
· *Plan B 2.0* – Lester Brown

2. The Need for Excitement and Creativity

Books
· *Tantra: The Art of Conscious Loving* – Charles and Caroline Muir
· *Love and Sexuality – Parts 1 and 2* – Omraam Mikhaël Aïvahov
· *Any book or audio program* by David Deida

Audio Programs
· *The Ultimate Relationship Program* – Robbins / Madanes

3. The Need for Individual Strength

Books
· *Maximum Achievement* – Brian Tracy
· *The Power of Focus* – Jack Canfield, Mark Victor Hansen and Les Hewitt
· *Way of the Peaceful Warrior (a novel)* – Dan Millman
· *Ask And It Is Given* – Ester and Jerry Hicks
· *The Road less Traveled* – M. Scott Peck M.D.
· *Your Erroneous Zones* – Dr. Wayne Dyer
· *The Greatest Salesman in the World (a novel)* – Og Mandino
· *The Holy Man (a novel)* – Susan Trott
· *Don't Sweat the Small Stuff* – Richard Carlson
· *Unlimited Power* – Anthony Robbins
· *Influence* – Robert B. Cialdini
· *The Prophet* – Kahlil Gibran
· *Think and Grow Rich* – Napoleon Hill
· *The Magic of Thinking Big* – David J. Schwartz
· *Feel the Fear and Do It Anyway* – Susan Jeffers
· *Turbo Coach* – Brian Tracy with Campbell Fraser
· *How to Win Friends and Influence People* – Dale Carnegie

- *Man's Search for Meaning* – Viktor E. Frankl
- *The Laws of Spirit (a novel)* – Dan Millman
- *Integral Psychology* – Ken Wilber

Audio Programs

- *The Psychology of Achievement* - Brian Tracy
- *Clarity* – Brian Tracy
- *Accelerated Learning Techniques* – Brian Tracy with Colin Rose
- *The Luck Factor* – Brian Tracy
- *The Ultimate Goals Program* – Brian Tracy
- *The Art of Exceptional Living* – Jim Rohn
- *Practical Wisdom* – Dan Millman
- *The Maverick Mindset* – Dr. John Eliot
- *The 11th Element* – Bob Scheinfeld
- *Lead the Field* – Earl Nightingale
- *The Strangest Secret* – Earl Nightingale
- *Unleash the Power within* - Anthony Robbins
- *The Power to Shape Your Destiny* – Anthony Robbins
- *Get the Edge* – Anthony Robbins
- *Personal Power 2* – Anthony Robbins

4. The Need for Love and Relationships

Books

- *Forgiveness: The Greatest Healer of All* – Gerald Jampolsky
- *Feel the Fear And Do It Anyway* – Susan Jeffers
- *Your Erroneous Zones* – Dr. Wayne Dyer
- *Self: I, Me, Mine, Ours, Illusions* – Yogi Shanti Desai
- *Spiral Dynamics* – Beck / Cowan
- *Boomeritis: A Novel That Will Set You Free (a novel)* – Ken Wilber
- *The Enneagram Made Easy* – Baron and Wagele
- *Destructive Emotions* – Dalai Lama and Daniel Goleman
- *Emotional Intelligence* – Daniel Goleman

· *Being Peace* – Thich Nhat Hahn
· *Further along the Road Less Traveled* – M. Scott Peck
· *A Path with Heart* – Jack Kornfield
· *The Art of Forgiveness, Loving Kindness and Peace* – Jack Kornfield
· *Tantra: The Art of Conscious Loving* – Charles and Caroline Muir
· *Love and Sexuality – Parts 1 and 2* – Omraam Mikhaël Aïvahov
· *The Prophet* – Kahlil Gibran
· *The Holy Man (a novel)* – Susan Trott

Audio Programs
· *The Ultimate Relationship Program* – Robbins / Madanes

5. The Need for Expression and Contribution

Books
· *NLP – The Technology of Achievement* - Steve Andreas and Charles Faulkner
· *Using Your Brain for a Change* – Richard Bandler
· *How to Win Friends and Influence People* – Dale Carnegie
· *Awaken the Giant within* – Anthony Robbins
· *How to Speak – How to Listen* – Mortimer J. Adler

Audio programs
· *The Secrets of Great Communicators* – Peter Thompson

6. The Need for Wisdom and Growth

Books
· *A Theory of Everything* – Ken Wilber
· *A Brief History of Everything* – Ken Wilber
· *Sex, Ecology, Spirituality* – Ken Wilber
· *The Story of Philosophy* – Will Durant
· *Lessons of History* – Will Durant

· *Heroes of History* – Will Durant
· *Modern Man In Search of a Soul* – C.G. Jung
· *The Paradox of God and the Science of Omniscience* – Clifford A. Pickover
· *The Basic Works of Aristotle*
· *Spiral Dynamics* – Beck / Cowan
· *Reality Here and Now* – Yogi Shanti Desai
· *Man's Search for Meaning* – Viktor E. Frankl
· *Discover Your Genius* – Michael J. Gelb
Audio programs
· *Kosmic Consciousness* – Ken Wilber

7. The Need for Spirituality

Since the need for spirituality is the pinnacle of the seven human needs, I will provide quite a substantial reading list in this category. Do not become daunted at the sight of this list. Start with whatever book you find most appealing and work from there. The reading list will reflect my background in yoga philosophy and yoga practice. However I will recommend books from various origins so that most everyone will find material to suit their inclinations in this area. Remember to keep an open mind.

Books
· *Hatha Yoga Practice Manual* – Yogi Shanti Desai
· *Yoga: Holistic Practice Manual* – Yogi Shanti Desai
· *Meditation Practice Manual* – Yogi Shanti Desai
· *Reality Here and Now* – Yogi Shanti Desai
· *Self: I, Me, Mine, Ours, Illusions* – Yogi Shanti Desai
· *Dynamic Balanced Living* – Yogi Shanti Desai
· *Personal to Global Transformation* – Yogi Shanti Desai

- *Sampoorna Yoga* – Yogi Hari
- *Holy Man (a novel)* – Susan Trott
- *How to Know God (Yoga Sutras)* - Swami Prabhavananda and Christopher Isherwood
- *Bhagavad-Gita* – (Isherwood/Prabhavananda or the version by Gandhi)
- *The Sermon on the Mount According to Vedanta* – Swami Prabhavananda
- *Siddhartha (a novel)* – Herman Hesse
- *Upanishads* – Eknath Eashwaran
- *What is a Spiritual Master?* - Omraam Mikhaël Aïvahov
- *The Powers of Thought* - Omraam Mikhaël Aïvahov
- *Harmony and Health* - Omraam Mikhaël Aïvahov
- *Bliss Divine* - Swami Sivananda
- *Complete Works* - Swami Vivekananda
- *How to Know God* – Deepak Chopra
- *Moments of Christ* – John Main
- *Open Mind, Open Heart: The Contemplative Dimension of the Gospel* – Father Thomas Keating
- *A Path with Heart* – Jack Kornfield
- *After the Ecstasy, the Laundry* – Jack Kornfield
- *Being Peace* - Thich Nhat Hahn
- *No Death, No Fear* – Thich Nhat Hahn
- *The Heart of the Buddha's Teaching* – Thich Nhat Hahn
- *Vows and Observances* – Gandhi
- *Autobiography* - Gandhi
- *Freedom in Exile* - The Dalai Lama
- *How to Practice* – The Dalai Lama
- *The Laws of Spirit (a novel)* – Dan Millman
- *No Boundary* – Ken Wilber
- *The Essential Ken Wilber*
- *Grace and Grit* – Ken Wilber

- *One Taste* – Ken Wilber
- *A Theory of Everything* – Ken Wilber
- *Holy Science* – Swami Sri Yukteswar
- *Autobiography of a Yogi* – Paramahansa Yogananda
- *Where there is Light* – Paramahansa Yogananda
- *Conversations with God – Books 1, 2 & 3* – Neale Donald Walsch

Audio programs
- *Kosmic Consciousness* – Ken Wilber

Most of the books can be found through www.amazon.com (or through the personal websites of the authors). The audio programs can be found through www.nightingaleconant.com and www.soundstrue.com.

Visit **www.sevenhumanneeds.com** for more resources.

The Author

"When I stand before God at the end of my life,
I would hope that I would not have a single bit of talent left,
and could say, "I used everything you gave me.""
– Erma Bombeck, writer

Gudjon Bergmann was born on December 24, 1972 in Reykjavik, Iceland. He is already an experienced writer, yoga teacher, speaker and entrepreneur. Before he began his career as an author, he translated five books from English to Icelandic (including titles by Dan Millman, James Redfield and Gerald Jampolsky), and spent just under five years writing as a part time journalist for a nationally published newspaper. He has written dozens of articles about health and philosophy in Icelandic magazines and newspapers and in his early twenties he also had a two-year career in the government-run radio in Iceland. To date he has written six books in Icelandic (see bibliography).

Gudjon Bergmann has studied and practiced yoga since 1997. His teachers have been Asmundur Gunnlaugsson, Yogi Shanti Desai and Shri Yogi Hari. He is a registered yoga teacher (500 hrs) with Yoga Alliance and for the last five years he has run a successful yoga studio in Iceland, where he has also trained just under 30 yoga teachers with Yogi Shanti Desai. To learn more about his yoga teaching visit www.sampoornayoga.com.

In the year 2000 Gudjon Bergmann hosted 30 half hour yoga shows on television that were re-run for just over two years in Iceland. In 2001 he was also the host of another very successful reality-based TV series on the tantric approach to relationships. His DVD *Yoga with Gudjon Bergmann* was the first of its kind in Iceland and is still available in English and Icelandic on PAL format.

The Seven Human Needs is his first book in English. It is also available as an audio book (see www.sevenhumanneeds.com). He is married to Johanna Boel Bergmann Hearn and together they have a son named Daniel Logi Bergmann. He is also stepfather to Bara Steinunn Jonasdottir, Johanna's daughter from a previous relationship. Gudjon Bergmann currently works as a writer, yoga teacher and speaker in Iceland and abroad.

Bibliography

· *Yoga for Beginners* (*Jóga fyrir byrjendur* – 2001)
· *Balance through the Chakras** (*Jafnvægi í gegnum orkustöðvarnar* – 2002)
· *Yoga and Sports* (*Jóga og íþróttir* – 2002)
· *Quit Smoking and Be Free** (*Þú getur hætt að reykja* – 2003)
· *Health, Happiness and Peace of Mind** (*Hreysti, hamingja, hugarró* – 2004)
· *Health, Happiness and Peace of Mind* – workbook (*Hreysti, hamingja, hugarró - vinnubók* – 2005)

*Available soon in English through www.amazon.com and www.booksurge.com.

Other material

· *Relaxation* CD (*Slökun* – 2001) – sold out
· *Yoga with Gudjon Bergmann* DVD (*Yoga með Guðjóni Bergmann* – 2004) – available in Icelandic/English PAL format

· *The Seven Human Needs* (audio book)
  – available through www.sevenhumanneeds.com

The Universal Prayer
– by Swami Sivananda

O, adorable Lord of mercy and love
Salutations and prostrations unto thee
Thou art omnipresent, omnipotent and omniscient
Thou art Satchidananda
Thou art existence, knowledge and bliss absolute
Thou art the indweller of all beings
Grant us an understanding heart, equal vision,
balanced mind, faith, devotion and wisdom.
Grant us inner spiritual strength
to resist temptation and to control the mind.
Free us from egoism, lust, anger, greed,
hatred and jealousy.
Fill our hearts with divine virtues.
Let us behold thee in all these names and forms.
Let us serve thee in all these names and forms.
Let us ever remember thee.
Let us ever sing thy glories.
Let thy name be on our lips.
Let us abide in thee forever and ever.

Om shanthi, shanthi, shanthi (peace, peace, peace)

461256

Made in the USA